# Pupil Book 3

Written by Ruth Atkinson, Andrew Jeffrey,
Adella Osborne, Louise Pennington, Romey Tacon
and Dr Tony Wing

4 points per bag

8 points per bag

OXFORD

# Contents

# How to use this book

Welcome to Numicon Pupil Book 3.

I'm Tia.

My name is Ben.

I'm Molly.

## Coloured sections

You will notice that the sections of this book are coloured red, yellow, blue, green or purple.

Each colour shows a different maths theme:

I'm Ravi.

Here are some of the things you will find inside this book.

**Pattern and Algebra**

**Numbers and the Number System**

**Calculating**

**Geometry**

**Measurement**

In this book you can try out new methods for finding answers...

... and think about how different maths ideas are connected.

## Practice

These questions help you to practise and explore the new maths ideas you have learned.

## Going deeper

These questions give you extra challenge and make you think deeply.

You will need to work with a partner on questions that have this symbol.

Your teacher may give you a photocopy master to use for questions with these symbols.

When you see this grey symbol, you can do these activities in the Explorer Progress Book.

### Glossary

There is a glossary of maths words in the back of the book. In the glossary, you can look up the meaning of words you don't know.

# Exploring all the combinations of numbers to 10

## Practice

1 a How many of the adding facts on this track total 7?

  b Can you find any other ways of making 7?

2 a How many adding facts on the track have a total of 9?

  b What other ways can you find to make 9?

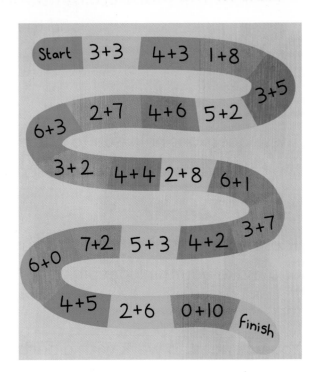

Start  3+3   4+3   1+8

3+5

6+3   2+7   4+6   5+2

3+2   4+4   2+8   6+1

6+0   7+2   5+3   4+2   3+7

4+5   2+6   0+10   finish

······································································

## Going deeper

1 Look at questions 1 and 2. Can you explain to your partner how you know you have found all the ways of making 7 and 9?

2 Which Numicon Shapes will you need to show all the combinations for making 8 with two numbers?

3 What could these two missing numbers be, if the total is less than 13?

3 + ▮ = ▮ + 8

# Subtracting numbers from 10 and below

## Practice

1 Look at the subtractions on this track.

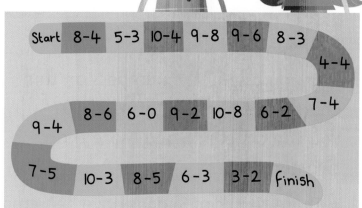

a How many are subtracting from 6?

b Are there any other subtractions from 6 you can do?

2 a How many are subtracting from 8?

b Are there any other subtracting from 8 facts that you can write?

Start  8 – 4  5 – 3  10 – 4  9 – 8  9 – 6  8 – 3

4 – 4

9 – 4  8 – 6  6 – 0  9 – 2  10 – 8  6 – 2  7 – 4

7 – 5  10 – 3  8 – 5  6 – 3  3 – 2  Finish

## Going deeper

1 Can you pair any of the adding and subtracting facts below together?

3 + 4 = 7   2 + 6 = 8   5 – 4 = 1   8 – 6 = 2   7 – 3 = 4   4 + 1 = 5

2 Look at the calculations below. Can you write a rule for each one that would help you with similar calculations?

a 4 + 0      b 1 + 8      c 7 – 0

d 8 – 4      e 2 + 5      f 6 – 5

# Exploring adding strategies

Sam shows facts of 10 with Numicon Shapes and number rods.

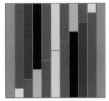 

## Practice

1 Can you use all the numbers on this chart once to make totals of 10? You can choose to add more than two numbers.

| 5 | 1 | 4 | 3 |
|---|---|---|---|
| 3 | 6 | 2 | 4 |
| 1 | 4 | 2 | 5 |

2 a These Numicon Shapes have been made into a rectangle. What is the total value of the Shapes?

b Can you build some rectangles using five different Numicon Shapes? Now calculate the totals.

..................................................................................................

## Going deeper

1 Decide which way you will add 6 + 15 + 4. Can you explain why?

2 Can you estimate who has the highest score below? Explain to your partner how you estimated this, then check your estimates.

| Name | Game scores | Total |
|---|---|---|
| Sam | 2, 6, 8, 4, 9 | ? |
| Ann | 5, 3, 6, 7, 5 | ? |
| Asmat | 1, 6, 9, 10, 5 | ? |
| Zara | 7, 5, 10, 4, 3 | ? |

# Solving number puzzles

For each puzzle, you can use any number from 1 to 10 only once. You need to make each line total the target number.

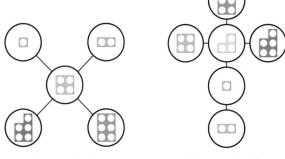

Target: 11     Target: 12

## Practice

1  Can you use Numicon Shapes to help you solve these puzzles?

a
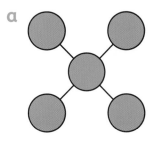
Target: 14

b
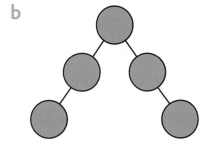
Target: 15

## Going deeper

1  a  You can use any number from 1 to 10 only once. What is the smallest and the largest total you can make on this pattern?
The total for each line must be the same.

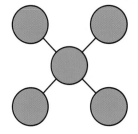

b  The rules change so you can use the same number twice. What is the smallest and largest number you can make now?

# Finding how many by grouping in 10s and 100s

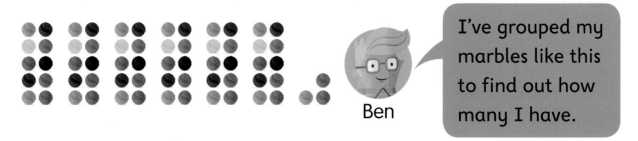

Ben

I've grouped my marbles like this to find out how many I have.

## Practice

1 Take turns to get a handful of counters. Can you estimate how many you have and use Ben's method to check? How close were your estimates?

2 Choose apparatus and use it to make these missing numbers. Can you write the missing numbers in numerals and words?

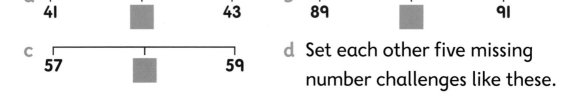

a 41 ▮ 43

b 89 ▮ 91

c 57 ▮ 59

d Set each other five missing number challenges like these.

## Going deeper

1 How many different ways can you show the number of marbles in Ben's collection? You can use writing, drawing and different apparatus.

2 Can you make up your own estimating problem?

# Exploring a Tens and Ones frame

**Tia's number of stickers**

| Tens | Ones |
|------|------|

**Ravi's number of stickers**

| Tens | Ones |
|------|------|

## Practice

1 Can you work out how many stickers Ravi collected?

2 Can you compare Tia and Ravi's number of stickers:

   a Who has fewer in the ones column?

   b Who has more tens?

   c Can you say who has more stickers in total?

......................................................................................

## Going deeper

1 Use Numicon Shapes to build a 2-digit number that has 5 tens. Which other 2-digit numbers can you build that have 5 tens? How can you be sure you have found them all?

2 Mike saved up to buy these trainers. He thought they cost £26·00.

Does he have enough money? How could you explain what has happened?

£62

# Finding how many beyond 100

I've collected 127 shells.

## Practice

1 Use counters to show how Ravi could group his shells, to check how many he has. Can you write down how many hundreds, how many tens and how many ones he has?

 2 Can you write these missing numbers in numerals and words?

a  132  □  134     b  249  □  251

c Now set your partner four missing number challenges like these.

## Going deeper

1 The children have a bag of coins. Ben's estimate is 164 coins, Ravi's estimate is 200. The actual number is 170. Ben says his estimate is closer. Do you agree? Explain why.

2 A cake for a 'Guess the weight of the cake' competition weighed 550 g. Ravi guessed 450 g, Tia guessed 600 g, Ben guessed 500 g and Molly guessed 525 g. Who won the cake?

# Exploring a Hundreds, Tens and Ones frame

**Molly's shell collection**

| Hundreds | Tens | Ones |
|----------|------|------|
|          |      |      |

**Ben's shell collection**

| Hundreds | Tens | Ones |
|----------|------|------|
|          |      |      |

## Practice

1 Molly said she had more shells than Ben. Do you agree? Can you explain?

2 Use these numbers:   5   2   8

  a What is the highest number you can make? What is the lowest?

  b Can you make the numbers that come between the highest and the lowest?

........................................................................................

## Going deeper

1 Can you explain the value of the counters in this HTO frame?

| Hundreds | Tens | Ones |
|----------|------|------|
|          |      |      |

2 Collect ten counters and a hundreds, tens and ones place value frame. Can you find:

  a the highest 3-digit number you can show

  b the lowest 3-digit number you can show

  c the lowest 2-digit number you can show?

# Using adding facts of 10 to find other adding facts

Josh has used 7 + 3 = 10 to help him solve 17 + 3.

## Practice

1 Which adding facts of 10 would you use to solve these?

   a 4 + 16 = 20    b 20 = 15 + 5    c 20 = 8 + 12    d 20 = 11 + 9

2 These number trios show a total of 10. If the total were 20, how would you adjust the other numbers to make them correct?

   Can you write your ideas as number sentences?

   a
   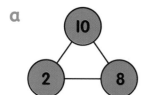

   b
   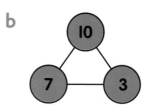

3 Can you copy and complete these number sentences? Write the adding fact of 10 that helps you.

   a ▢ + 5 = 70       b 31 + ▢ = 40       c 6 + 24 = ▢

..............................................................................................................

## Going deeper

1 Without calculating, can you spot which of these calculations give a total of 20? Explain to your partner how you know.

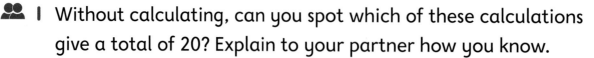

3 + 18      16 + 4      4 + 15      3 + 17

12 + 7      16 + 3      8 + 12

# Finding all combinations for teen numbers

Ellen is using Numicon Shapes to show combinations of two numbers that equal 15.

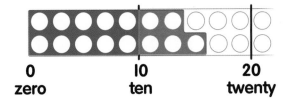

| 0 | 10 | 20 |
|---|---|---|
| zero | ten | twenty |

## Practice

1 Can you find other combinations of two numbers that equal 15?

2 Here is the middle part of a subtracting pattern. Can you answer these calculations and then complete the pattern?

$16 - 8 = $ ▨

$16 - 9 = $ ▨

$16 - 10 = $ ▨

## Going deeper

1 a How can you adjust $9 + 6 = 15$ to show a total of 14?

b Work with your partner to make up similar adjusting challenges for each other.

2 What do you know that would help you to answer $17 - 3$?

3 What do you know that can help you to solve these calculations?

a $19 - $ ▨ $= 14$ 

b $18 = $ ▨ $+ 6$

4 If you know the fact $4 + 3 = 7$, what other adding calculations does this help you solve?

# Relating adding and subtracting below 10 to adding and subtracting for teen numbers

I want to find adding and subtracting facts for this number trio.

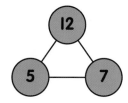

## Practice

1 Can you write the adding and subtracting facts that Tia can find?

2 Add 10 to two of the numbers in this trio. Can you write the new adding and subtracting facts?

3 Can you show ways of adjusting these to make the totals correct?

   a 4 + 5 = 19       b 3 + 1 = 14       c 2 + 3 = 15

## Going deeper

1 Luca is saving up for a new game which costs £18. He has saved £12.

   a How much more does he need to save?

   b Can you write this as a number trio?

   c Which calculation should he use? 18 + 12 or 18 − 12?

2 The children had a one hour lunch break. They spent half the time on the field and half on the playground. Which number sentences and number trio can you make to show this? What do you notice?

# Solving missing number problems

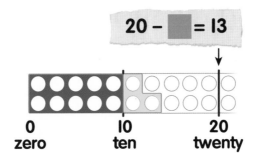

$$20 - \boxed{\phantom{0}} = 13$$

0
zero

10
ten

20
twenty

## Practice

1 Which adding fact could help you solve the problem above?

2 Which facts can help you to solve these?

a  $20 - 11 = \boxed{\phantom{0}}$

b  $\boxed{\phantom{0}} + 8 = 20$

c  $20 - \boxed{\phantom{0}} = 6$

d  $20 = \boxed{\phantom{0}} + 17$

e  $15 = \boxed{\phantom{0}} - 5$

f  $9 = 20 - \boxed{\phantom{0}}$

## Going deeper

1 Can you explain how you would solve $32 + \boxed{\phantom{0}} = 40$ and $32 = 40 - \boxed{\phantom{0}}$ ?

2 Phil is running a 20 km race. He has run 11 kilometres.

a How much further does he have to run?

b Can you explain which of these number sentences you would use to show this and why?

$11 + \boxed{\phantom{0}} = 20$     $20 - \boxed{\phantom{0}} = 11$     $20 - 11 = \boxed{\phantom{0}}$

3 Yusef bought a pen that cost 60p. He paid with a £1 coin.

a Can you show how to calculate his change?

b Which coins might he receive in his change?

# Exploring hundreds, tens and ones

Milk cartons come in packs of 10.

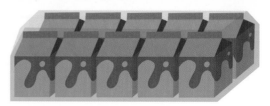

## Practice

1 Can you use cubes or number rods to show how many packs of milk will be needed for these children to get a carton each?

    a 80 children          b 50 children          c 70 children

2 Look at these multiples of 10. Can you write them as 2-digit numbers and in words?

    a 6 tens             b 9 tens             c 4 tens

........................................................................

## Going deeper

 1 Can you write two lists of 10 numbers that would go in this set diagram?

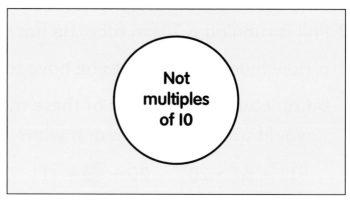

Numbers < 101

Not multiples of 10

 2 Can you work out how many packs of milk you would need to open to give out these numbers of cartons?

    a 24         b 59         c 81         d 18         e 126

# Exploring multiples of 10 further

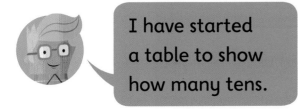

I have started a table to show how many tens.

| Number | Number of 10s |
|--------|---------------|
| 100 | 10 |
| 110 | 11 |
| 120 | 12 |
| 130 | |
| | |

## Practice

 1 Can you copy and continue Ben's table? Discuss what patterns you can see. Can you explain how the digits change?

2 Can you write how many tens are in these numbers?

   a 190   b 240   c 750   d 80   e 610   f 330

## Going deeper

1, 2, 4, 6, 7, 9, 0, 0, 0, 0

1 a Can you make different multiples of 10 using all the numerals in this list? You can only use each numeral once.

b Now compare your numbers and read each other's numbers aloud.

c Agree how many tens there are in each of your numbers.

# Exploring base-ten apparatus

The milk is delivered to Eva's school in boxes. Each box holds 100 cartons of milk.

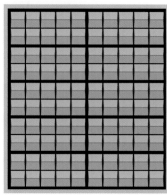

## Practice

1 How many ways can you find to show the 100 milk cartons with base-ten apparatus?

2 Take turns to read a number below out loud. Can you show it with apparatus on a HTO frame?

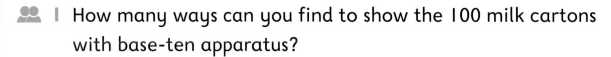

| 178 | 460 | nine hundred | 304 | fifty-six | 222 |

3 How many cubes are needed to cover these numbers of 100-flats from the base-ten apparatus?

   a 5          b 9          c 7          d 4

..................................................................................................

## Going deeper

1 Paul and Lia both measure the same cupboard. Paul uses sixteen 10-sticks to measure it. Lia uses 1-cubes. How many 1-cubes does she use?

2 Can you decide whether this HTO frame is correct? If not, what could you do to correct it?

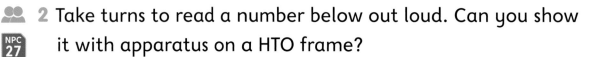

| Hundreds | Tens | Ones |
|----------|------|------|
| 3 | 5 | 6 |

# Exploring hundreds, tens and ones

I've noticed that there are 24 tens and 3 ones in 243.

| Hundreds | Tens | Ones |
|---|---|---|
| | | |

## Practice

 1 Take turns to choose numbers from this list.

195, 241, 759, 586, 612, 443

Can you say how many tens and how many ones are in them?

2 Can you write a number:

a 100 more than 723    b 200 less than 339    c 10 more than 207

d 10 less than 524    e with more 100s than 648?

## Going deeper

 1 How many hundreds, tens and ones are there in 469? How else could you describe it using hundreds, tens or ones?

2 ⬤ = 100    ⬤ = 10    ⬤ = 1

a Can you write the number shown by these counters?

b If there were 5 more yellow counters, what number would it be?

c If you double your answer to **question b**, what is your total?

d Take turns to set each other challenges like these.

# Exploring adding, subtracting and equivalence

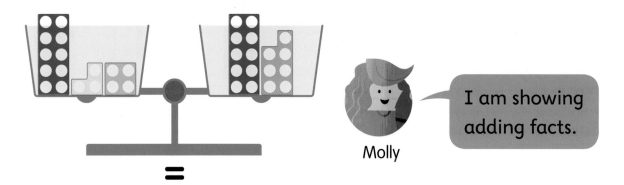

Molly

I am showing adding facts.

## Practice

1 Which number trios can you write for Molly's adding fact?

2 Can you write the related adding or subtracting facts for these calculations?

| 18 − 4 | 12 + 7 | 16 − 9 | 14 + 5 | 2 + 15 |

| 19 − 3 | 13 + 5 | 17 − 5 | 16 − 11 | 4 + 12 |

## Going deeper

1 If you found all the number trios for 19, how many would there be?

2 Jake and Una put their savings together to buy a model that cost £12. Jake pays £5.

a Can you draw a number trio to show how much Una pays?

b Can you make up your own problem for the trio?

# Relating adding and subtracting facts

Lucy has adjusted the numbers in one trio to make
two new trios.

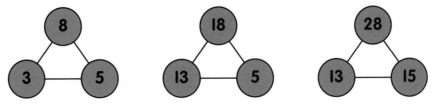

## Practice

 1 Talk about how Lucy has adjusted the numbers.

2 Can you write the adding and subtracting facts for Lucy's
last trio?

3 Can you draw a trio to show 4 + 5 = 9? Now can you adjust
the trio to make two new trios?

## Going deeper

 1 Work together. Can you find out what the missing number
could be for each of these number trios?

a 18, 14, ▢          b ▢, 5, 11

2 Ben says both these additions have the same total.
Can you explain why?

11 + 17 = ▢          17 + 11 = ▢

3 Ben says the sets of numbers below are related. Do you agree?
Can you explain why?

12, 7, 5          32, 17, 15

# Recording families of related facts

Tia

I want to see how many related facts I can find for this number trio.

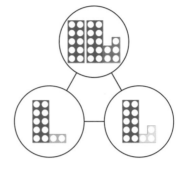

## Practice

1 How many related facts can Tia find?

2 Can you write or draw the missing number from this trio?
Next explore how many related facts you can find.

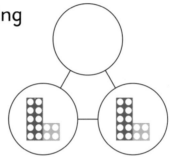

.....................................................................................................

## Going deeper

 1 Why do you think there are fewer related facts for the trio you explored in question 2 than for question 1?

2 Do you think these calculations are correct? Can you explain?

$$23 - 25 = 48 \qquad 25 - 23 = 48$$

3 Can you find number trios for these problems?
What do you notice?

George counts 18 cars on the first day and 21 on the second.
How many cars does he count altogether?

A car park has 39 spaces. In the morning, cars fill 21 spaces.
How many more cars can park there?

# Solving empty box number problems

Sanjay used a pan balance to help him solve adding problems.

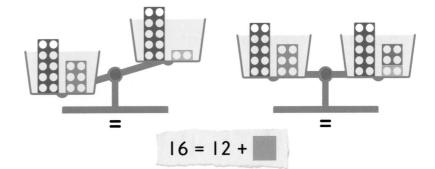

16 = 12 + ▢

## Practice

1 Decide how you will work out and complete these number sentences together.

a 24 + ▢ = 29    b ▢ + 23 = 27    c ▢ + 24 = 30

d 26 = 23 + ▢    e 28 = ▢ + 6    f 27 = 12 + ▢

## Going deeper

1 a Can you complete this calculation and show it in a number trio?

26 = ▢ + 12

b What other missing number problems can you write for this trio?

2 Can you make number trios using these numbers? Are there any numbers you can't use?
Compare your ideas. What do you notice?

25, 3, 13, 38, 32, 18, 5, 15, 8

# Keeping count

Ben and Tia found different methods of keeping count of the bikes in a race.

## Practice

1 Ben used counters to show there were 145 bikes in the race. How many counters do you think were in each pot?

2 For a week, the class kept a tally chart of the number of birds visiting the garden. Can you copy and complete it?

| Days of the Week | Tallies | Total |
|---|---|---|
| Monday | ЖНТ ЖНТ ЖНТ ЖНТ ЖНТ ЖНТ II | |
| Tuesday | | 25 |
| Wednesday | | 36 |
| Thursday | ЖНТ ЖНТ ЖНТ ЖНТ ЖНТ III | |
| Friday | | 19 |

## Going deeper

1 Can you explain which method you would use to count the number of lengths a swimmer swims in a pool?

2 Aisha says most children in her class prefer football to tennis. Can you find out if this is true for your class?

# Exploring number lines

Alfie records counting in 10s on an empty number line.

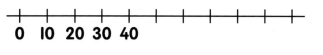

0  10  20  30  40

## Practice

1 Which numbers are missing from these number lines?

a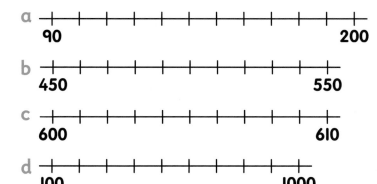

90                    200

b
450                   550

c
600                   610

d
100                   1000

2 Joe has eighteen 10-rods and six 1-rods. Which number will they reach if he lays them in a number rod track?

## Going deeper

1 Talk about which numbers you think could be missing from these number lines.

a
130                    b
                       550

2 Matt found that the 0–100 cm number line fits along $\frac{1}{2}$ of the length of a table.

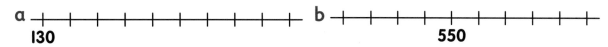

a How long was the table in metres?

b How many 10-rods would fit along it?

c How many 5-rods would fit along it?

# Exploring an abacus

Amir's class found they could
keep count of their marbles on
an abacus.

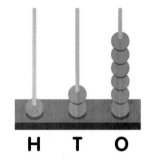 

H   T   O

## Practice

 1 Can you draw abacuses like the one above to show these
numbers?

746,   593,   444,   68,   86,   515

2 Play a game with number cards from 1 to 10 and an
 abacus. Take turns to turn over a number card and add that
number onto the abacus. The first player to reach 200 wins.

## Going deeper

1 Can you work out the highest number you could show on a HTO
abacus like the one above? How many counters would you need?

2 How many different numbers could you show on the abacus with
 five counters? Experiment together. What rules will you set?

3 Astrid says this shows 374.
Is she correct? Can you explain
your answer?

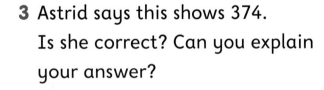

| Hundreds | Tens | Ones |
|----------|------|------|
|          |      |      |

# Zero as a place holder

Heidi experiments by putting 0 in different places on the hundreds, tens and ones (HTO) frame.

| Hundreds | Tens | Ones |
|---|---|---|
| ▦ | | |
| I | 0 | 0 |

| Hundreds | Tens | Ones |
|---|---|---|
| | ▮ | |
| 0 | I | 0 |

| Hundreds | Tens | Ones |
|---|---|---|
| | | ▪ |
| 0 | 0 | I |

## Practice

I Take turns to choose a number from the list below. Can you make it with base-ten apparatus on a HTO frame? Find two ways to change it into a 100s number using a zero. Can you show the new numbers with apparatus?

62,   37,   14,   83,   26,   59

..................................................................................................

## Going deeper

I James was born on the second of January, two thousand and seven. How could you write this in numerals?

2 Usha measures how many steps she takes during the day.

Look at the numbers on her step counter below. How would each total change as she takes the next step? What if she takes 10 more steps?

a 0001          b 0009          c 0089          d 0119

e 0240          f 0499          g 0709          h 0999

# Bridging multiples of 10 when adding

Ravi adds 6 and 7 using Numicon Shapes.

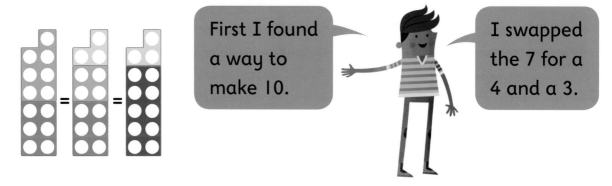

First I found a way to make 10.

I swapped the 7 for a 4 and a 3.

## Practice

1 Can you talk about and show different ways of adding 6 and 7 together? Choose any apparatus you need.

2 Choose a number from List A and from List B. Can you use Ravi's method to add them together? Try this three times.

| List A | List B |
|--------|--------|
| 9 | 6 |
| 8 | 5 |
| 7 | 4 |

## Going deeper

1 Agree how you will solve 6 + 8 = ▮ + 10.

2 Can you explain how you will solve this problem? How can you check your answer?

> Ravi plants 135 bean seeds, then Molly plants another 8. How many bean seeds have they planted altogether?

# Adding 9

I have two methods for adding 9.

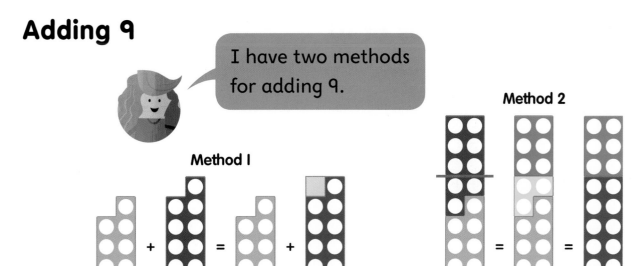

Method 1

Method 2

## Practice

1 Molly's first method is to add 10 instead of 9. Then she adjusts the total to make it one fewer. Can you use this method to add 9 to these numbers?

23, 47, 172, 384, 96

2 Molly's second method is to reach the next multiple of 10, by adding part of the 9. Then she adds the remaining part of the 9. Can you use this method to add 9 to these numbers?

28, 39, 256, 465

## Going deeper

1 Look at a 100 square together. Can you explain what happens when you add 9 to any number?

2 Can you change these calculations to make them correct?

   a 43 + 9 = 50 + 1      b 376 + 9 = 380 + 6

3 Try adding 108 + 9 using both of Molly's methods. Which do you find easiest to calculate and which do you find easiest to explain?

# Bridging multiples of 10

I've used an empty number line to show bridging 10.

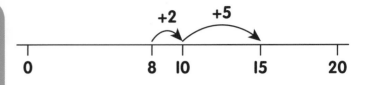

## Practice

1  Choose a number from List A and from List B to add together.
   Can you draw number lines to show your calculations?
   Try this three times.

   **A:** 15, 46, 77, 88

   **B:** 6, 7, 8, 9

2  Can you write balancing number sentences for these number rods?

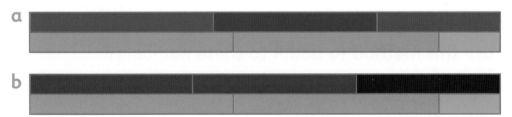

a

b

............................................................................................

## Going deeper

 1  Can you use number rods to show your solution to 126 + 7?

2  Can you write the number sentences shown on this number line?

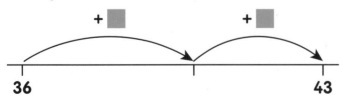

# More bridging and adding lists of numbers

I added 7, 6 and 9. Then I used number rods to check my total.

## Practice

 1 Choose three or more of the number cards below and calculate the total. Take three turns each. Talk about the methods you use.

Can you find different number sentences each time?

6  7  8  9  10

2 Can you copy and complete these balancing number sentences?

a  67 + 8 = 70 + ▢    b  5 + 98 = ▢ + 100    c  150 + ▢ = 147 + 9

d  416 + 7 = ▢ + 3    e  4 + ▢ = 8 + 326

## Going deeper

 1 Can you explain how knowing 48 + 6 helps you calculate 48 + 46?

2 Can you explain how to reach from 157 to 165 in two steps?

# Exploring subtracting strategies

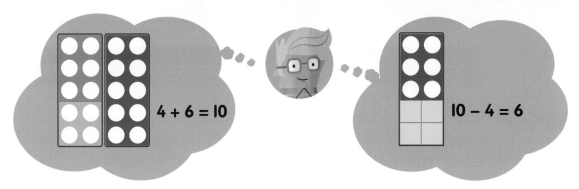

## Practice

1 Can you write subtracting sentences for these calculations?

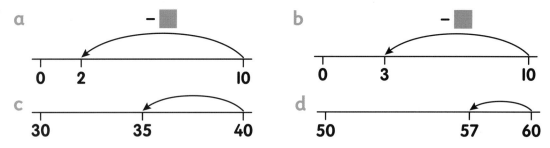

2 Group the subtracting facts that are connected.

| 20 – 7 | 620 – 7 | 495 – 2 | 350 – 7 | 760 – 6 | 290 – 2 |

| 406 – 6 | 90 – 2 | 490 – 2 | 60 – 6 | 120 – 7 | 460 – 6 |

........................................................................................................

## Going deeper

1 Can you explain how knowing 70 – 4 helps you to calculate 170 – 4 and 570 – 4?

2 Can you explain how you will complete these number sentences?

a ▮ – 7 = 43          b ▮ – 5 = 165

# Subtracting a single-digit number

I have found a way of subtracting 6 from 14.

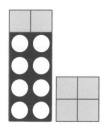

## Practice

 1 Can you explain how Ravi has subtracted 6 from 14?

2 Can you choose a number from List A and subtract it from a number in List B? Use number rods or Numicon Shapes to help you and write your calculations as number sentences. Try this four times.

**A:** 6, 7, 8, 9    **B:** 12, 13, 14, 15

## Going deeper

 1 Do you think Ravi's method would work if you are calculating 215 – 7? Talk about your ideas.

2 Can you write an empty box calculation for this problem?

There are 7 coats left at the end of a clothes sale. 6 have been sold. How many coats were there to start with?

3 Can you make up a problem for this empty box calculation?
23 – ▮ = 5

# Bridging multiples of 10 when subtracting

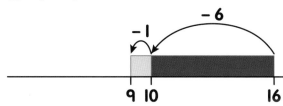

I have shown subtracting with rods on an empty number line.

16 – 7 = 9

## Practice

1 Can you subtract numbers in List A from numbers in List B? Show your calculations on empty number lines.

**A:** 6, 7, 8, 9

**B:** 34, 13, 42, 285

2 Can you write the number sentences shown on these number lines?

a
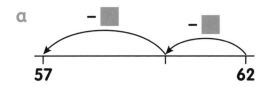

b
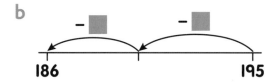

..................................................................................................

## Going deeper

 1 Can you make up a problem that uses the calculation in 2a?

2 Bria said she only used 63 – 7 to answer the subtraction 463 – 7. Can you explain why?

# Subtracting 9

I have two methods for subtracting 9.

**Method 1**     **Method 2**

17 – 9 = 8

## Practice

1 Talk about how to use Tia's methods to answer 26 – 9.

2 Tia's first method is to subtract part of the 9 to reach the previous multiple of 10. Then she subtracts the rest of the 9.

Can you use this method to subtract 9 from these numbers?

25,   57,   174,   93

3 Tia's second method is to subtract 10 instead of 9 and adjust the answer by adding 1.

Can you use this method to subtract 9 from these numbers?

28,   139,   56,   65,   382

## Going deeper

1 Zahra writes 53 – 9 = 54 – 10. Is she correct? Explain your reasoning.

2 Can you complete these and explain what you notice happening when you subtract 9?

a  41 – 9 = ▢        b  84 – 9 = ▢        c  167 – 9 = ▢

# Exploring multiples

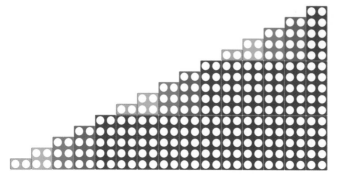

This sequence uses multiples of 2. The 10-Shape is the 5th number in the sequence.

## Practice

1 Can you work out the position of these numbers in the sequence?

16, 24, 32, 40, 62

2 Can you complete this statement?

Multiples of 2 will always _____.

3 Can you complete these sequences?

a 888, , 886, , , 883,     b 221, ■, ■, 218, ■

## Going deeper

1 Use a sorting diagram to sort these 3-digit numbers into **Multiples of 2** and **Not multiples of 2**.

342, 836, 469, 110, 728, 287, 694, 121, 392, 704

2 How many multiples of 2 are between 12 and 20 (including 12 and 20)? What about 42 and 50? Try 112 and 120. Can you explain to your partner what you notice?

# Exploring sequences of multiples of 3, 4 and 8

I am building sequences of multiples of 3, 4 and 8.

## Practice

1 Can you copy and complete these sequences?

a 36, ▧, 42, 45, ▧, 51, ▧, ▧

b 99, ▧, ▧, 90, 87, ▧

c 117, ▧, 123, 126, ▧, ▧

2 Draw a Venn diagram with two overlapping rings. Label one **Multiples of 2** and the other **Multiples of 3**. Can you use the diagram to sort these numbers?

15, 28, 6, 94, 56, 27, 24, 123, 136, 72

3   20, 12, 36, 28, 8, 40, 32, 4, 48, 16, 44, 24

a What multiples are shown in this list?

b Choose numbers to show the sequence for multiples of 8.

## Going deeper

1 Can you explain whether or not all multiples of 3 will be odd numbers?

2 Can you work out which multiple of 4 and 8 comes between 60 and 70? Explore this together.

# Exploring sequences of multiples of 5 and 10

I am going to sort multiples of 5 on this Carroll diagram.

|  | Multiple of 5 | Not multiple of 5 |
|---|---|---|
| Odd |  |  |
| Not odd |  |  |

## Practice

1 Draw your own diagram like Tia's and sort these numbers.

25, 12, 49, 26, 50, 51, 35, 48, 34, 17, 75, 40, 120, 125

2 What would the 13th step in the sequence of multiples of 5 be?

## Going deeper

1 Are these statements correct? Can you explain your ideas?

20 is the 4th step in the sequence of multiples of 5.
20 is the 2nd step in the sequence of multiples of 10.

2 Hita saves 10p coins, Rob saves 5p coins. They have both saved the same amount. Could both of them have saved £1·25? Can you explain why?

3 How many multiples of 5 are there between 0 and 50? Can this help you find how many there are between 0 and 100?

# Finding sequences on the 100 square

## Practice

1 Look at this 100 square. Can you find the missing numbers and name the sequence on the yellow squares?

2 Can you colour a pattern for the multiples of 8 sequence on a 100 square? What do you notice about the pattern?

| 1 | 2 | 3 | 4 | 5 | 6 | 7 | 8 | 9 | 10 |
|---|---|---|---|---|---|---|---|---|---|
| 11 | 12 | 13 | 14 |  | 16 | 17 | 18 | 19 | 20 |
|  | 22 | 23 | 24 | 25 | 26 | 27 | 28 | 29 |  |
| 31 | 32 | 33 | 34 | 35 |  | 37 | 38 | 39 | 40 |
| 41 | 42 | 43 | 44 | 45 | 46 | 47 |  | 49 | 50 |
| 51 | 52 | 53 |  | 55 | 56 | 57 | 58 | 59 | 60 |
| 61 | 62 |  | 64 | 65 | 66 | 67 | 68 | 69 | 70 |
| 71 |  | 73 | 74 | 75 | 76 | 77 |  | 79 | 80 |
| 81 | 82 | 83 |  | 85 | 86 | 87 | 88 | 89 |  |
| 91 | 92 | 93 | 94 | 95 | 96 | 97 | 98 |  | 100 |

## Going deeper

1 Can you explain the sequences shown on these number squares? Can you find the missing numbers?

a

|  | 28 |  | 32 |
|---|---|---|---|
| 24 | 22 |  |  |
| 10 | 12 |  | 16 |
|  | 6 | 4 | 2 |

b

| 25 |  | 15 | 10 | 5 |
|---|---|---|---|---|
| 30 | 35 |  | 45 | 50 |
|  | 70 | 65 | 60 |  |
|  | 85 | 90 |  | 100 |
|  |  |  |  | 105 |

2 Can you explain whether these statements are true or false?

   a 12 is not a multiple of 4.    b 30 is a multiple of 5.

   c 24 is a multiple of 3.       d 18 is not a multiple of 2 and 3.

# Perpendicular, horizontal and vertical lines

Hazel is exploring the vertical and horizontal lines in her name with geo strips.

## Practice

1 a How many vertical strips are there in Hazel's name?

b How many horizontal strips are there?

2 Can you use geo strips to make your name in capital letters? How many vertical and horizontal strips are there?

3 Can you list five capital letters with horizontal and vertical lines that are perpendicular to one another?

## Going deeper

1 Can you make a word that has:

a fewer vertical and horizontal strips than 'Hazel'

b more vertical and horizontal strips than 'Hazel'?

2 Which letter is described by these instructions?

Place a strip horizontally. Then place a strip vertically down, so that it is perpendicular from the centre point of the horizontal strip.

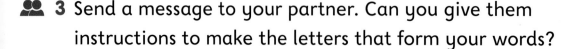 3 Send a message to your partner. Can you give them instructions to make the letters that form your words?

# Exploring parallel lines

Ravi has made a rectangle on a geo board with an elastic band.

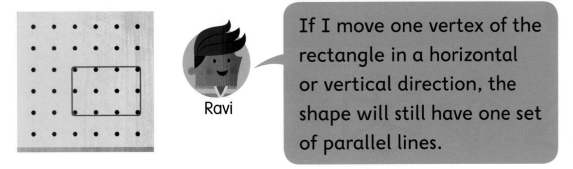

Ravi

If I move one vertex of the rectangle in a horizontal or vertical direction, the shape will still have one set of parallel lines.

## Practice

1 **a** Can you explore Ravi's statement? Is he correct?

GMS 7

    **b** What new shapes can be made by this move? Can you draw them on dotty paper and name them?

GMS 7

2 Can you make or draw three polygons that have no parallel lines?

GMS 7

3 Can you make or draw a shape that has more than two sets of parallel lines?

......................................................................................

## Going deeper

GMS 7

1 Can you move one vertex of Ravi's rectangle to make a shape that has no parallel lines but still has a set of sides that are perpendicular?

2 Can you move two vertices of Ravi's rectangle to make a shape that has parallel lines but no perpendicular lines?

3 Can you choose sorting criteria and sort all the shapes you created in the Practice questions?

# Building 3D shapes

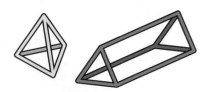
Here are some skeleton 3D shapes.

## Practice

1 Can you use straws or pipe cleaners to make the roof of this building as a skeleton shape?

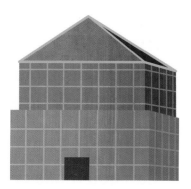

2 Liam has 12 straws. What 3D skeleton shapes can he make using exactly 12 straws? Can you find four different shapes?

3 Can you make a 3D skeleton shape which has a face that is shaped like a pentagon? How many straws will you need?

## Going deeper

1 Kayla uses 18 straws and 12 balls of modelling dough. Can you predict what 3D skeleton shape this could make and then test out your ideas?

2 Secretly make a 3D skeleton shape using straws and modelling dough. Take it apart and give your partner the pieces. Will the model they make be the same as yours?

# Investigating faces, edges and vertices

I've explored 3D shapes and have found that Faces + Vertices − Edges = 2.

## Practice

1 How many faces, edges and vertices does a square-based pyramid have? Does this fit Molly's statement?

2 Can you test out Molly's statement further by exploring other shapes? Find two more examples that fit Molly's statement.

3 If Molly's statement is true, can you work out what shape she has made with 4 faces and 4 vertices? How many edges will it have?

## Going deeper

1 An octahedron has 8 faces and 12 edges. Can you predict how many vertices it will have?

2 Can you make a 3D model with 9 edges and 6 vertices? How can you use Molly's statement to help you?

# Revising multiplying as repeated adding

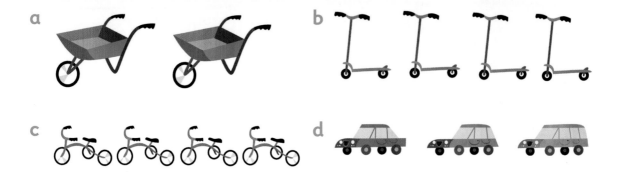

a    b

c    d

## Practice

1 Look at the pictures with each letter above. Can you write repeated adding sentences to show the total number of wheels for each group?

2 Can you write 5 × 0 as an adding sentence?

........................................................................

## Going deeper

1 Four children have each saved £3 of their pocket money.

Can you explain which of these number sentences shows this?

   4 + 4 + 4    3 + 4    3 × 3 × 3 × 3    4 × 3    3 + 3 + 3 + 3

2 Can you make up your own multiplying number story for these Numicon Shapes?

# Using the word 'times' and finding the product

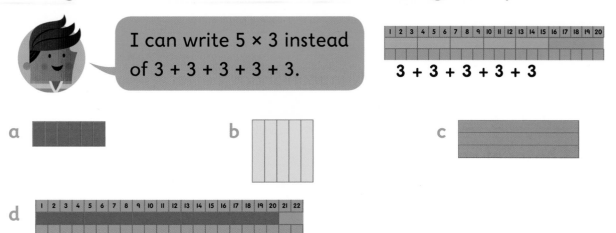

I can write 5 × 3 instead of 3 + 3 + 3 + 3 + 3.

3 + 3 + 3 + 3 + 3

a

b

c

d

## Practice

1 Can you write a repeated adding sentence for each group of apparatus?

2 Now can you write the multiplying number sentence for each group of apparatus?

3 Use apparatus to show how you will find these products. Can you write the complete number sentences?

   a 7 × 2 = ▨    b 6 × 5 = ▨    c 5 × 4 = ▨    d 8 × 3 = ▨

..................................................................................................

## Going deeper

1 Draw a puppet design that uses different numbers of sticks, buttons and feathers. Four children want to make it.

How many of each item will they need? Write down the repeated adding and the multiplying number sentences for each item. Also try this for any other equipment you think they need.

# More multiplying

## Practice

 1  Some foods are packed in Numicon Shape patterns. Agree the multiplying sentences you will write for each of these:

    a  3 boxes of eggs

    b  2 packs of yoghurts

    c  4 packs of apples

    d  1 pack of tomatoes.

2  Some foods come in bags. Can you use apparatus to help you calculate how many of each fruit there are?

    a  3 bags       b  4 bags

........................................................................................................

## Going deeper

1  What do you notice happening when you multiply by 1?
Can you make up a rule and show some examples?

2  Take turns to choose a multiplying instruction and make up a multiplying shopping problem for your partner to solve.

    4 × 3     2 × 6     5 × 4     1 × 5     3 × 4     7 × 2

# Knowing when to multiply

There are 6 children in a hoop race. Each child needs 3 hoops.

I can show this with Numicon Shapes and number rods.

0 zero      10 ten      20 twenty

## Practice

1 Can you write two number sentences to show the total number of hoops needed?

2 Choose apparatus and write two number sentences to calculate how much equipment is used for these races.

a 4 children each balancing 8 beanbags.

b A stilts race for 6 children. Each child needs 2 stilts.

## Going deeper

 1 Each day, the breakfast club uses these items:

| | | |
|---|---|---|
| 10 eggs | 3 packets of butter | 4 loaves of bread |
| 5 boxes of cereal | 8 litres of milk | 2 jars of spread |

How much of each item do they need for 5 days? Which number sentences do you prefer to write for this and why?

2 Can you write these as multiplying sentences?

2 + 2 + 2 + 4          3 + 3 + 9 + 3

# Making arrays and writing multiplying sentences

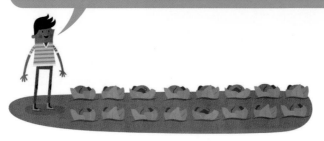

I've planted these lettuces in an array.

## Practice

1 Can you write a multiplying sentence for Ravi's array?

2 Can you write multiplying sentences for these arrays?

3 Can you draw arrays for these multiplying calculations and write the complete multiplying sentences?

a 2 × 6 = ▮      b 5 × 4 = ▮      c 3 × 8 = ▮

## Going deeper

1 Are there any other arrays for 16 that Ravi could have used when he planted his lettuces? Draw your ideas.

2 Amber says there are six arrays for 12.
How could she prove this?

# Exploring the commutative property of multiplying

I can rotate my array and I can show it with number rods.

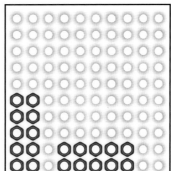

## Practice

1 Which two multiplying sentences can you write for Molly's arrays?

2 Build each of these arrays yourself and write the multiplying sentence. Now rotate them. Can you write the commutative multiplying sentences?

a 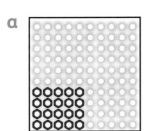  b 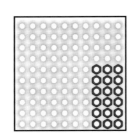  c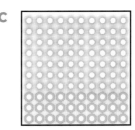

3 Can you show 6 × 3 with number rods? Work out the commutative multiplying sentence and show it with rods.

## Going deeper

 1 Are any of these arrays connected? Can you explain your reasoning?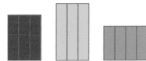

2 Can you explain how you will find commutative multiplying sentences if the product is 18?

# Using multiplying facts when solving problems

## Practice

 1 Explore this grid to find five pairs of commutative facts.

| | | | |
|---|---|---|---|
| ▬ | 5 × 5 | ⦿⦿⦿⦿⦿⦿⦿⦿ | 10 × 3 |
| ⊞ | 9 × 2 | ▭ | ⊞ |
| 7 × 3 | ▬▬▬▬▬ | ⦿⦿⦿ | ▬▬▬ |

2 10 pairs of children go to school assembly. They sit on benches that seat 10. How many benches will they need?

......................................................................................

## Going deeper

1 Can you solve these empty box problems?

a 4 × 0 = ▨ × 4      b ▨ × 5 = ▨ × 7      c 3 × 1 = ▨ × ▨

2 Can you explain how you solve this problem?

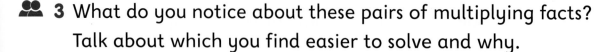

The 6 Jones children each have 4 meatballs for lunch.
The 4 Smith children each have 6 meatballs for lunch.
Do both families need the same number of meatballs?

3 What do you notice about these pairs of multiplying facts?
Talk about which you find easier to solve and why.

a 10 × 7 = ▨ or 7 × 10 = ▨      b 5 × 6 = ▨ or 6 × 5 = ▨

# Exploring the associative property

I can multiply more than two numbers. Four times two three times.

4 × 2 × 3

4 × 2    4 × 2    4 × 2

1 2 3 4 5 6 7 8 9 10 11 12 13 14 15 16 17 18 19 20 21 22 23 24 25

## Practice

1 Use number rods to build 3 × 2 × 4. Can you compare it with Molly's number sentence? What do you notice?

2 Tom and Lin each baked 5 buns. They use 4 cherries to decorate each bun. Show this with number rods. Write a multiplying sentence to show how many cherries are needed.

## Going deeper

1 Molly says that 2 × 3 × 10 has the same product as 10 × 2 × 3.

   a Do you agree? Can you explain your answer?

   b Can you use these numbers to find other multiplying sentences with the same answer?

2 What do you notice about these calculations? Can you find any other multiplying calculations that relate to them?

   2 × 40        10 × 4 × 2

# Exploring dividing problems

I can find how many 5s are in 20 using Numicon Shapes and number rods.

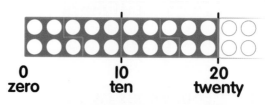

## Practice

1 Can you use Molly's method to answer these questions?

a How many £2 toys can you buy for £16?

b
$$3\overline{)\,1\ \ 8}$$

2 Can you complete these dividing number sentences?

a 14 ÷ 2 = ☐    b 60 ÷ 10 = ☐    c 24 ÷ 3 = ☐

................................................................................

## Going deeper

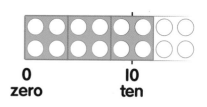

 1 a Which dividing sentences explain this picture?

How many 4s in 12?    12 divided into 4s.    12 divided by 4.

b Can you use the ⌐ and ÷ symbols to show two dividing number sentences for the picture?

c Can you make up a dividing story for the picture?

# Finding 'how many tens' in different multiples of 10

Freddie uses Numicon Shapes and coins to show how many 10p coins there are in 50p.

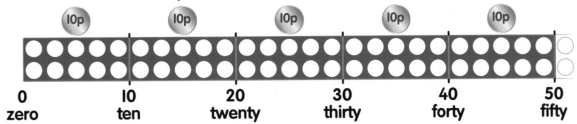

## Practice

1 Can you use Freddie's method to find how many 10p coins are in these amounts?

   a £1·50    b £1    c 70p    d £2

2 Write dividing sentences to show how many tens are in:

   a 30    b 100    c 20    d 90    e 80

3 Can you write a dividing and multiplying sentence for this?

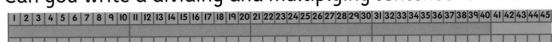

## Going deeper

1 What number is missing from this dividing number trio? How many multiplying and dividing sentences can you find for this trio?

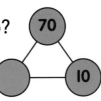

👥 2 a How are these two calculations connected? Talk about this and what you know that helps you to complete them.

$$\boxed{\phantom{0}} \div 10 = 9 \qquad 9 \times \boxed{\phantom{0}} = 90$$

b Can you draw the number trio for these calculations?

# Solving dividing problems

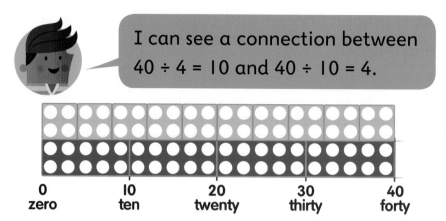

I can see a connection between
40 ÷ 4 = 10 and 40 ÷ 10 = 4.

## Practice

1 Can you find connected dividing calculations for these?

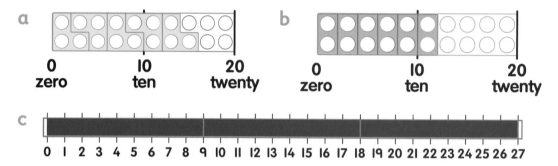

2 Can you complete these dividing calculations? Write the multiplying facts that help you.

a 20 ÷ 5 = ☐        b 18 ÷ 2 = ☐        c 16 ÷ 4 = ☐

## Going deeper

1 Can you complete this family of multiplying and dividing facts? Now explain how you did this and draw the number trio.

8 × 5 = ☐        40 ÷ ☐ = 8        5 × ☐ = ☐        ☐ ÷ 8 = ☐

2 Work out a number trio and family of multiplying and dividing facts where the largest number is 24.

# Introducing remainders – how many are left over?

I find how many 5s are in 32 and get a remainder of 2.

I can write it like this: $5\overline{)32}$ with $6r2$

or as $32 \div 5 = 6\ r2$.

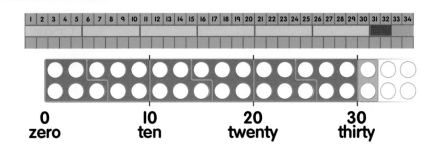

| 0 | 10 | 20 | 30 |
| zero | ten | twenty | thirty |

## Practice

1 Can you find out how many 5s there are in these numbers and if there is a remainder? Write number sentences to show your answers.

   a 17    b 36    c 24    d 40    e 43    f 22

2 Four children have a packet of 30 balloons to share. How many balloons do they have each? How many will be left?

## Going deeper

1 How could you write the dividing calculation shown here?

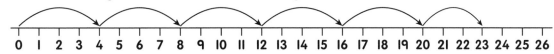

2 What is the highest remainder you could have if you are dividing by 5? Can you explain why?

3 Can you explain which numbers will never have a remainder when you are dividing by 10?

# Making journeys using quarter turns

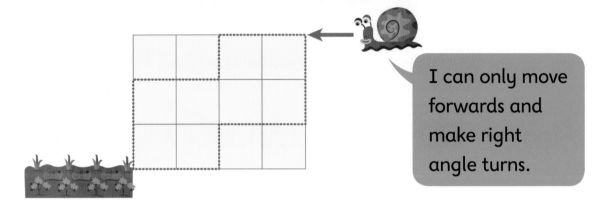

I can only move forwards and make right angle turns.

## Practice

 1 The snail needs to follow the trail to the vegetables and back to where it started. Can you write instructions for it to follow? Can you predict how many turns it will make?

2 Next time, the snail makes 10 turns to get to the vegetables and back. Can you draw this new trail and write the instructions for it?

## Going deeper

1 The snail needs to go to the vegetables from where it started. What is the least number of quarter turns it can make? Can you say how you know and write the instructions?

2 What different hexagon trails can you make? Write your instructions for three different hexagons. What do you notice about the number of turns for each?

# Linking turns and angles

Molly and Ravi are making
angles using pipe cleaners.

## Practice

1  a Can you describe Molly's angle?

   b What can you say about Ravi's angle?

2  a Can you use a pipe cleaner to make a right angle?

   b Can you make an angle bigger than a right angle?

   c Can you make an angle smaller than a right angle?

   d Compare your angles with your partner and organize
     them from smallest to largest.

3 At 3 o'clock, what angle do the clock hands make?

## Going deeper

1  The angle between the two hands on this clock is
   a right angle. At what time will the hands next
   make a right angle? Explain your thinking.

2 Give your partner a time when the angle between the
   hands is a right angle. Then choose a number of quarter
   turns for the minute hand. What will the new time be?
   Explain to each other how you can work it out.

# Angles in triangles and four-sided shapes

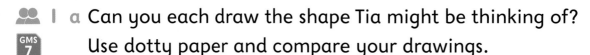

> I'm thinking of a shape.

> It has 1 right angle and 2 angles smaller than a right angle.

## Practice

1  a Can you each draw the shape Tia might be thinking of? Use dotty paper and compare your drawings.

   b Can you draw another example of the same kind of shape?

2 Draw your own triangle, but keep it hidden. Describe the angles to your partner. Can they work out what your triangle might look like?

3 Try question 2 again for a polygon with 4 angles.

........................................................................................................

## Going deeper

1 Hadi has made a shape that contains 2 right angles, 1 angle bigger than a right angle and 1 angle smaller than a right angle. Draw a possible shape that Hadi could have made.

2 Can you draw and name some quadrilaterals where opposite angles are equal? How many can you find?

# Regular and irregular polygons

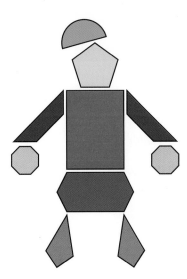

## Practice

1 Which polygons in the picture are regular? Explain how you know.

2 Can you make or draw your own polygon person, made entirely of regular shapes?

3 Now change each polygon slightly, so that each polygon becomes irregular. What do you change each time?

## Going deeper

1 Ben says the red part of the body is a regular polygon. Can you explain why he is not correct?

2 How would you explain what makes a shape regular to a friend?

3 Can you make or draw a regular shape that has:

    a all angles smaller than a right angle

    b all right angles

    c all angles bigger than a right angle?

# Partitioning 2- and 3-digit numbers

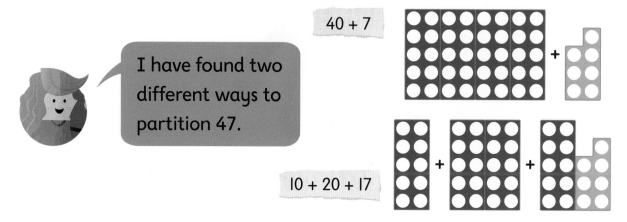

I have found two different ways to partition 47.

40 + 7

10 + 20 + 17

## Practice

1 Can you find more ways to partition 47?

 2 Can you find ways of partitioning these numbers?

    a 58                 b 232

Compare your ideas with your partner. How many different ways have you found?

## Going deeper

1 Can you copy and complete these calculations?

    a 30 + 26 = ▢ + 36         b ▢ + 40 = 69 + 20

2 How can you partition these numbers so that each part has two digits? Find different ways then compare these with your partner.

    a 75 = ▢ + ▢ + ▢ + ▢       b ▢ + ▢ + ▢ = 184

# Exploring amounts

Raj used apparatus and place value cards to represent amounts of money.

| Hundreds | Tens | Ones |
|---|---|---|
| | | |
| £1 | 10p 10p 10p | 5p |

1 3 5

## Practice

1 Talk about other ways you could show these amounts.

    £6·23        b £4·69        c 394p        d 241p

2 Which of these amounts are equivalent?

  £8·19   £3·73   373p   602p   £7·10   819p   £6·20   710p   £6·02

## Going deeper

1 Can you explain how to solve these empty box problems?

  a $180 - \boxed{\phantom{0}} = 100$       b $\boxed{\phantom{0}} - 60 = 300$

  c $507 - \boxed{\phantom{0}} = 500$       d $\boxed{\phantom{0}} - 5 = 900$

2 What different amounts of money could this HTO frame show? Can you give examples of other measures it could show?

| Hundreds | Tens | Ones |
|---|---|---|
| | | |
| 1 | 2 | 3 |

# Finding different ways to make the same amount

This machine only accepts 5p, 10p, 20p and 50p coins.

## Practice

1 Which coins could Ben use to buy a snack costing 85p?

2 Can you find two ways to make these amounts?

   a £1·54     b £1·77     c £2·45     d 89p     e £4·16

## Going deeper

1 Elsie gives her 3 grandchildren £25 to share equally. She gives them a £20 note and £5 note. Which notes and coins do they need to exchange the notes for to share it? Will there be any money left over?

2 Rob had £1·63 but he has dropped some coins. He now has a £1 coin, a 10p and a 1p coin. If he had seven coins to start with, which coins did he drop?

# Solving problems with partitioning

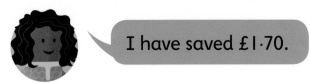

I have saved £1·70.

## Practice

1 What is the smallest number of coins Tia could have?

2 Which items do you think Tia could not buy with her money?

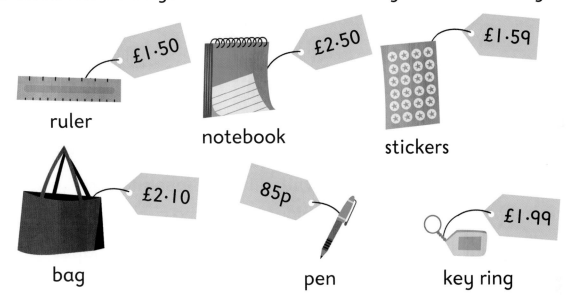

ruler £1·50

notebook £2·50

stickers £1·59

bag £2·10

pen 85p

key ring £1·99

3 Ed has also been saving. He has saved one of each coin.
Can you say how much money he has saved?

## Going deeper

1 A parking meter takes 5p, 10p, 20p, 50p and £1 coins.
The charge is 70p an hour. Claire wants to park for 3 hours.
Which coins do you think she can use?

2 The school buys glue in 50 ml, 100 ml and 250 ml containers.
Each class has 500 ml. Which combinations of containers
could they have?

# Sorting shapes using a Venn diagram

Sara has some triangles and quadrilaterals.
She sorts her shapes using this Venn diagram.

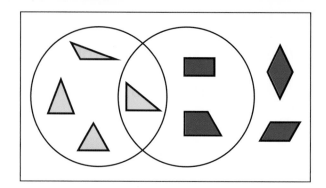

## Practice

1 Can you work out what labels Sara used to sort her shapes?

2 Can you draw a Venn diagram with different labels to sort Sara's shapes? Put at least one shape where the circles overlap.

3 Draw two large circles or use hoops. Then draw four shapes each on squared paper and cut them out.

 Can you make a Venn diagram and use it to sort your shapes?

## Going deeper

1 Can you draw one more shape for **each section** of Sara's Venn diagram?

2 a Make a Venn diagram. Use eight 2D or 3D shapes and label **each section** using a sticky note.

 b Hide your labels. Can your partner work out how you sorted the shapes?

# Sorting shapes using a Carroll diagram

Elsa has sorted her 3D shapes using this Carroll diagram.

|  | 6 faces | Not 6 faces |
|---|---|---|
| 8 vertices | | |
| Not 8 vertices | | |

## Practice

1 a Can you work out which two shapes Elsa has placed incorrectly? Explain your reasoning.

 b Can you explain where the two shapes should go?

2 Look at the top left section of the diagram. Can you draw or name another 3D shape that could go here?

3 Using the shapes on the diagram above, can you make your own Carroll diagram with different labels? Ask your partner to check they are all placed correctly.

## Going deeper

1 Otis says, "Only cuboids will go in the top left section." Is he right? Can you explain?

2 Make your own Carroll diagram using your own labels. Can you put at least one 3D shape in every section?

# Making a tree diagram to sort shapes

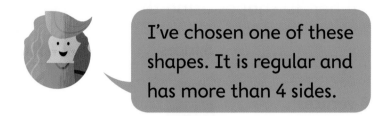

I've chosen one of these shapes. It is regular and has more than 4 sides.

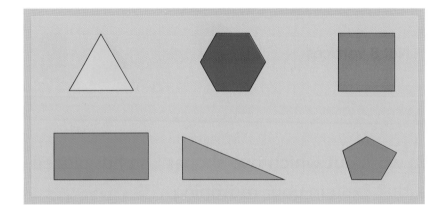

## Practice

1 Can you work out which shape Molly picked?

2 a Can you draw a tree diagram to show how to identify Molly's shape?

  b How can you continue your diagram so that it will sort all of the regular shapes above?

## Going deeper

1 Can you suggest a different shape that would also fit the description "regular with more than 4 sides"?

2 Can you make a tree diagram for a selection of 3D shapes?

# Sorting 2D shapes based on symmetry

Bilal has made shapes using square and triangular tiles and sorted them.

|  | Quadrilateral | Not a quadrilateral |
|---|---|---|
| **Symmetrical** |  |  |
| **Not symmetrical** |  |  |

## Practice

1 Can you make an extra shape for each part of Bilal's diagram? Use square and triangular tiles.

2 a Can you make your own sorting diagram that uses "symmetrical" as one of the labels? It could be a tree, Venn or Carroll diagram. Use pattern blocks to make 6 shapes and sort them.

   b Hide the other labels from your partner. Can they work out what these are? Can they add two more shapes?

## Going deeper

1 Emma sorts the shapes below into a Venn diagram. All the shapes fit inside the circles using **two** criteria. What could her criteria have been? Can you draw the Venn diagram?

a

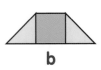
b

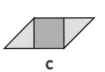
c

d

e

f

# Ordering numbers

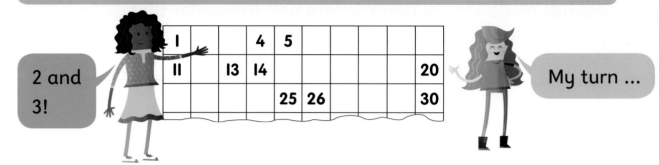

2 and 3!

My turn ...

## Practice

1 Can you find where these pairs of numbers should go on an empty 100 square?

27   28        63   73        50   51        42   62

2 Take turns to choose other pairs of numbers for your partner. Can you explain how you know where to place them?

3 Can you use an empty 16 square to find out where these numbers should go?   5   11   16

····································································

## Going deeper

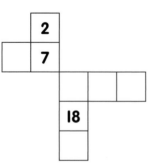

1 These numbers are part of a number square. Can you work out which number square they belong to?

2 Use an empty 100 square. If 100 is in the top left hand corner, can you explain where number 1 will be?

3 Try putting 100 in another corner. Discuss what has happened to any patterns you noticed.

66

# Comparing heights and lengths

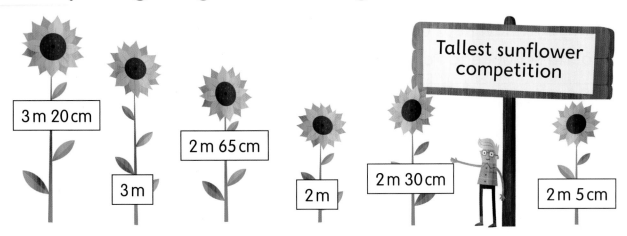

## Practice

1 Can you write the height of all these sunflowers in centimetres?

2 Choose four sunflowers and compare the heights using **>** and **<**.

3 Try to find the height of the third shortest sunflower.

## Going deeper

1 Lucy's mum needs 7m 50cm of carpet for the stairs. The carpet shop has carpets for sale in the following lengths:

740 cm     780 cm     8 m     760 cm

   a   Which pieces would be long enough?
   b   Can you say which piece is the best one to buy?

2 Can you suggest what the missing digits might be, to complete these 3-digit numbers so they are in order? Two of the numbers should have a difference of 200.

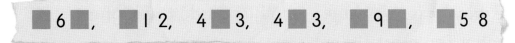

■6■,   ■12,   4■3,   4■3,   ■9■,   ■58

# Ordering 3-digit numbers

Molly and Ravi kept a record of how many steps they walked around school each day with a pedometer.

|  | Monday | Tuesday | Wednesday | Thursday | Friday |
|---|---|---|---|---|---|
| Molly | 793 | 645 | 985 | 839 | 876 |
| Ravi | 569 | 782 | 953 | 891 | 974 |

## Practice

1 Which day did Ravi walk the furthest?

2 Can you say who took fewer steps on Friday?

3 Who walked the closest number of steps to 1000 in one day?

4 Write Molly's daily numbers of steps in order, using the **>** symbol.

........................................................................................

## Going deeper

1 All the runners in a race wear a number.
Discuss what you think the organizers need to
do to check that everyone finishes the race.

2 Can you explain the rules you follow to put 3-digit
numbers in order? Write these with you partner.

3 Play 'Make the highest number' ten times.
   • Shuffle two packs of 0–9 number cards.
   • Put the cards face down and take three cards each.
   • Make the highest possible number with your cards.
   • The winner is the player who has made the highest
     number the most times.

# Working with number lines

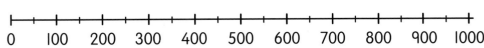

Having fifties and hundreds on the number line helps me to find number ranges.

| | | | | | | | | | | | |
0   100   200   300   400   500   600   700   800   900   1000

## Practice

1 Tia was disappointed to find the pages 434–441 were missing from her book. How many pages were missing?

2 Choose a number range for each of these pairs of numbers.

| 8   49 | 73   99 | 121   134 | 156   182 |

 3 Can you explain to your partner how to correct these?

    a  827 > 872          b  486 falls in the range 301–399

## Going deeper

1 Choose different number ranges for this empty number line.

| | | | | | | | | |
0

2 1750 cyclists in a bike ride set off in groups of 50. How many groups are there altogether?

Can you explain how to work this out? Talk about it with your partner.

# Adding and subtracting multiples of 10 and 100

The adding fact $4 + 5 = 9$ helps me answer $40 + 50$ and $400 + 500$.

## Practice

1 Can you copy and complete Molly's table?

| Adding and subtracting facts | | |
|---|---|---|
| Multiples of 10 | Numbers to 10 | Multiples of 100 |
| $40 + 30 = 70$ | $4 + 3 = 7$ | |
| | $5 - 1 = 4$ | |
| | | $900 - 700 = 200$ |
| | $1 + 8 = 9$ | |
| $70 - 60 = 10$ | | |

 2 Talk about which difference number sentence this shows. How will you write it?

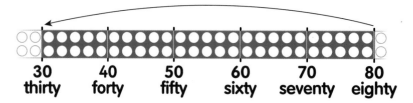

| 30 | 40 | 50 | 60 | 70 | 80 |
|---|---|---|---|---|---|
| thirty | forty | fifty | sixty | seventy | eighty |

## Going deeper

1 a How much less has Ravi scored than Tia in total?

b Can you use symbols to show the order of the total scores?

| Game scores | | |
|---|---|---|
| Child | Turn 1 | Turn 2 |
| Ben | 300 | 200 |
| Ravi | 400 | 400 |
| Tia | 300 | 600 |
| Molly | 200 | 500 |

c Can you make up other questions about the game scores?

2 Can you use a number line to show how you will solve this problem?

$$700 - \boxed{\phantom{00}} = 400$$

# Calculating change from multiples of 10 and 100

Knowing 5 + 5 = 10, helped me find change from £1·00.

I spent 50p.

## Practice

1 Can you write the number fact that helps you calculate the change for each of these?

   a Buying a £1·60 toy and paying with £2.

   b Buying a £5·80 toy and paying with £6.

   c Buying a £9·30 toy and paying with £10.

   d Buying a £4 toy and paying with £5.

## Going deeper

1 Ali spends £8·10 on shopping and pays with a £10 note. How will you calculate his change?

2 You could write this subtracting sentence as 100 subtract 80 equals 20. Can you find other ways to write the sentence by using different words?

$$100 - 80 = 20$$

 3 Talk about ways of solving this problem. Lena has £130. She puts £40 in her savings. How much does she have left to spend?

# Adding and subtracting multiples of 10

When I added a multiple of 10 to this 2-digit number, the ones didn't change.

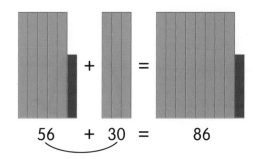

56 + 30 = 86

## Practice

1 Which adding fact helped Tia to do the calculation?

2 Can you subtract each number in List B from each number in List A?

**A:** 95    68    187

**B:** 30    50    40

## Going deeper

1 For each pair of highlighted numbers on the square, can you write:

a the subtracting sentence

b the fact that will help you

c the inverse adding sentence?

| 41 | 42 | 43 | 44 | 45 | 46 | 47 | 48 | 49 | 50 |
| 51 | 52 | 53 | 54 | 55 | 56 | 57 | 58 | 59 | 60 |
| 61 | 62 | 63 | 64 | 65 | 66 | 67 | 68 | 69 | 70 |
| 71 | 72 | 73 | 74 | 75 | 76 | 77 | 78 | 79 | 80 |
| 81 | 82 | 83 | 84 | 85 | 86 | 87 | 88 | 89 | 90 |
| 91 | 92 | 93 | 94 | 95 | 96 | 97 | 98 | 99 | 100 |

2 Talk about which digits will change and why as you solve this calculation.

146 + 30 = ▢

# Adding and subtracting multiples of 10 and bridging hundreds

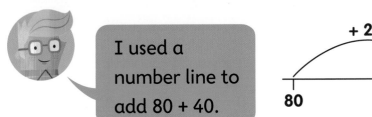

I used a number line to add 80 + 40.

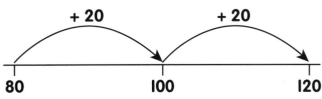

## Practice

1 Try using Ben's method to do these calculations.

a 70 + 80 = ▮

b 90 + 50 = ▮

c 140 – 60 = ▮

d 130 – 70 = ▮

## Going deeper

1 Which adding and subtracting calculations can you write for this number line?

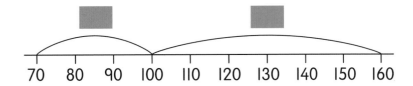

2 Talk about how to answer these questions. How will you show your methods?

Classes are collecting pennies.
Ali's class collects 700.
Ruby's collects 100 fewer than Ali's.
Leo's class collects 100 more than Ali's.

a How much did each class collect?

b What was the total number of coins collected?

c How many pounds were collected?

# Using patterns of similar calculations

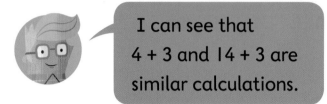

I can see that 4 + 3 and 14 + 3 are similar calculations.

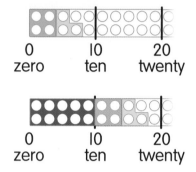

## Practice

1 Start with 49 – 46 = 3. Can you write a pattern of similar subtracting calculations that finishes with 9 – 6 = 3? Agree which digits you will change.

2 Look at the two smaller numbers in this trio. Can you change these to find other adding sentences with a total of 36?

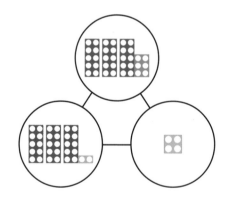

## Going deeper

1 a How does knowing the total of 4 + 5 help you answer 45 + 54? Can you find other adding facts that knowing this would help you answer?

  b Can you find other calculations using these patterns?

# Doubling, halving and near doubles

I can use Numicon Shapes to show doubling and halving.

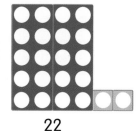

22

Half of 22 equals 11

## Practice

1 Can you double and halve these numbers?

**Numbers to double:** 14, 31, 26, 47     **Numbers to halve:** 46, 82, 70, 38

2 What doubling and halving questions could you write if:

a the answer is 10      b the answer is 24?

3 Max buys two toy cars. He pays with a £5 note. He gets £3·20 change. How much did each car cost?

## Going deeper

1 Mia says, "Double 32 equals 62." Is she correct? Can you explain your answer?

 2 Explain the different methods you could use to solve these.

a 24 + 25      b 38 + 37      c 19 + 18

3 Can you explain how you will solve this?

56 + ▮ = 113

# Adjusting numbers

I can sometimes make a calculation easier by adjusting the numbers.

## Practice

1 Can you show how to adjust the numbers in these calculations so you can solve them more easily?

a  83 − 29 = ☐    b  57 + 29 = ☐    c  96 − 49 = ☐

d  87 − 59 = ☐    e  269 + 25 = ☐    f  159 + 19 = ☐

2 Compare these equivalent calculations. Can you explain how they have been adjusted?

a  187 − 58 = 189 − 60    b  546 + 127 = 543 + 130

......................................................................................

## Going deeper

1 Can you adjust numbers in these calculations to write an easier equivalent calculation?

a  158 + 734 = ☐ + ☐        b  183 − 38 = ☐ − ☐

c  425 + 542 = ☐ + ☐        d  361 − 12 = ☐ − ☐

2 a When you are adjusting calculations to make numbers easier, what sort of numbers do you look for first?

b Could you make a general rule for how to adjust numbers in adding calculations?

c Is there a general rule for adjusting subtracting calculations?

# Reasoning to solve different problems

Work with your partner to think of different ways to solve these problems.

Choose the best strategy together, then find the answer.

## Practice

1 Lenny's family are going on holiday. They travel 240 miles on the first day and 240 miles on the second. How long was their journey?

2 A school hall seats 165 people. 187 people want to go to a concert there. How many can't have seats?

3 A charity raises £79 on a stall and £120 in a raffle. How much have they raised altogether?

4 Molly has 105 game cards. Ravi has 86. How many do they have altogether?

## Going deeper

1 a Can you write instructions to help someone solve a problem like this?

$$\blacksquare + \blacksquare = 28$$

b Can you explain whether your method for **question 1a** would work for an empty box problem like this?

$$\blacksquare + \blacksquare + \blacksquare = 34$$

# Exploring scales

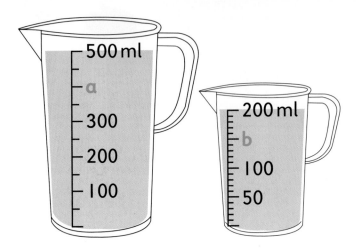

## Practice

1 Can you work out the missing number on each jug's measuring scale?

2 Maisie reads until 2:35 in the afternoon. Kyle reads until 2:50 in the afternoon. What is the difference in the length of time they read?

## Going deeper

1 Tom and Amar measure 200 ml of milk each using the two measuring jugs above. Could either of the measuring jugs be used to measure 140 ml? Can you explain your answer?

2 Can you explain a connection between the pattern of numerals in multiples of 10 and the pattern in multiples of 100?

3 Ben says he is showing 150 with these number rods. Do you agree? What other numbers could this show?

# Exploring intervals of 2 and 20

| Fruit | Number of children |
|---|---|
| Strawberry | 10 |
| Mango | 5 |
| Raspberry | 6 |
| Orange | 6 |
| Kiwi | 3 |

This table shows our favourite fruit.

## Practice

1 Can you draw a bar chart with intervals of 2 to show Tia's information?

2 Can you find the missing numbers in these sequences?

a 80, 100, ▮, 140, ▮, ▮, 200, ▮

b ▮, 420, ▮, 460, 480, ▮, ▮

3 Take turns to choose one of these cards showing multiples of 2. Change it into a multiple of 20. Can you explain the changes to the digits each time?

8   12   38   64   20   56

## Going deeper

1 The scale on a baby's bottle goes from 60 to 260. There are 9 intervals marked in between. Can you work out the size of the intervals and write the numbers on the scale?

79

# Exploring intervals of 5 and 50

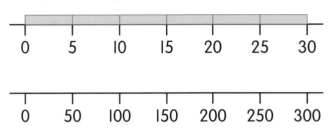

I'm looking for connections between multiples of 5 and multiples of 50.

## Practice

1 Molly saves one 5p coin and one 50p coin each week.
She has saved 75p in 5p coins and £7·50 in 50p coins. Can you write the sequences to show how her savings increased?

2 Can you draw a bar graph showing the data below from a traffic survey? Work together and decide which scale to use.

100 coaches, 250 vans, 50 motorbikes, 500 cars, 450 lorries

3 Can you add four more numbers to each part of this Carroll diagram? Draw your own diagram to show them.

|  | Multiple of 50 | Not multiple of 50 |
|---|---|---|
| < 499 | 350 | 205 |
| > 499 | 800 | 953 |

## Going deeper

1 How many multiples of 5 are there between 0 and 100? Explain how this helps you to work out how many multiples of 50 there are between 0 and 1000.

2 Using your bar chart from question 2, where would you plot 75 bicycles? Where would you plot 20 caravans?

# Exploring scales and intervals

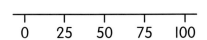

0    25    50    75    100

I can use number rods to show this scale.

## Practice

1  a Which number rods will Ben need to show the scale?

   b Now extend the scale to 200 and talk about the patterns you see.

   c Can you continue the pattern to 300 and beyond?

2 Can you find the missing numbers in these sequences?

   a 125, ▦ , 175, ▦ , ▦ , 250, ▦ , ▦

   b 475, ▦ , ▦ , 550, ▦ , 600, ▦

   c ▦ , 350, ▦ , 400, 425, ▦ , ▦

## Going deeper

1  A school wants to raise £1000 for books.
   So far, they have raised £500. They usually
   raise about £30 a week. What scale would
   you use on a graph to show how the
   savings grow?

2  What scale would you use for this graph?
   There are 28 children in Stork Class.

**Favourite colours in Stork Class**

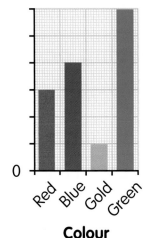

Number of children

0

Red  Blue  Gold  Green

**Colour**

# Finding halfway

I've used rods on this number line to show halfway between 0 and 10.

## Practice

 1 Can you use number rods and a number line to show halfway between these pairs of numbers?

  a  30 and 40        b  200 and 300        c  110 and 120

2 Talk about what the missing numbers on this table could be. Can you find one way to copy and complete it?

| Number | Halfway number | Number |
|--------|----------------|--------|
| ? | 85 | ? |
| ? | 130 | ? |
| 400 | ? | ? |
| ? | 345 | ? |

3 A swimming pool is 50 metres long. Children will swim half of its length in a race. How long is their race?

## Going deeper

1 a Can you find the two multiples of 10 closest to 65?

  b Explore to find other numbers that 65 is halfway between.

  c Can you explore the number 350 in the same way?

# Reading scales

a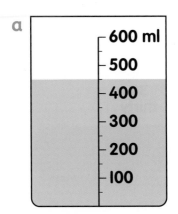

b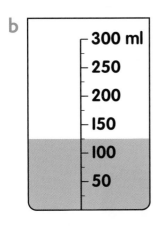

c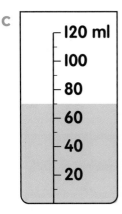

## Practice

1  Can you write the amount shown in each measuring jug?

2  a  Zak's measuring jug goes up to 250 ml, but he needs 500 ml of water for a recipe. How can he measure this?

   b  How could he measure 300 ml?

3  Kay is in a bike race. There are drink stations every 20 km. How far has Kay cycled when she reaches the sixth drink station?

......................................................................................................................................

## Going deeper

 1  a  Can you draw a graph to show this information?

   b  What questions could you ask about your graph?

| Football match ticket sales | |
| --- | --- |
| Day of the week | Number of tickets |
| Monday | 125 |
| Tuesday | 23 |
| Wednesday | 226 |
| Thursday | 90 |
| Friday | 165 |

# Rounding and estimating

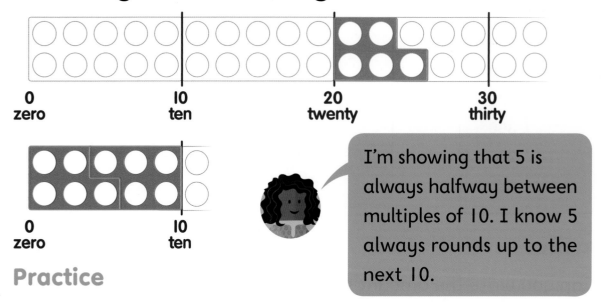

| 0 | 10 | 20 | 30 |
|---|----|----|----|
| zero | ten | twenty | thirty |

| 0 | 10 |
|---|----|
| zero | ten |

> I'm showing that 5 is always halfway between multiples of 10. I know 5 always rounds up to the next 10.

## Practice

1 Which numbers round to 30?

2 Can you round these numbers to the nearest 10 cm?

   a 4m 38 cm     b 3m 65 cm     c 2m 97 cm     d 3m 43 cm

 3 a Can you round the numbers below into these three sets?

| Rounds to 10 cm | Rounds to 50 cm | Rounds to 90 cm |
|---|---|---|

| 14 cm | 88 cm | 53 cm | 16 cm | 49 cm | 6 cm |
|-------|-------|-------|-------|-------|------|
| 91 cm | 97 cm | 45 cm | 12 cm | 59 cm | 83 cm |

   b Are there any numbers that don't fit into these sets?
   Can you explain why?

## Going deeper

1 Luca needs 20 ml of vanilla essence for a cake. He bakes
5 cakes. Should he buy a 75 ml, 120 ml or a 110 ml bottle
of vanilla essence?

# Rounding to the nearest 100

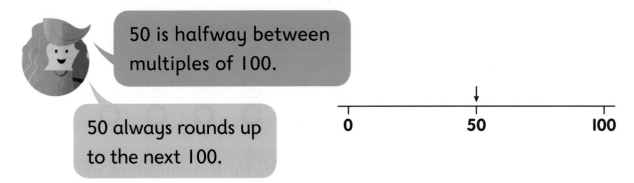

50 is halfway between multiples of 100.

50 always rounds up to the next 100.

## Practice

1 Can you write the range of numbers that round to 200?

2 Can you round these numbers to the nearest 100 cm?

　a 351 cm　　b 149 cm　　c 924 cm

3 Jay is baking. One recipe needs 150 g of flour, the other needs 400 g. Which bag of flour should he buy?

Flour 500 g　Flour 1 kg

## Going deeper

1 Which numbers go in each of these sets when rounded to the nearest 100 cm? Can you find four for each set?

| Rounds to 300 cm | Rounds to 700 cm | Rounds to 1000 cm |

2 Can you use rounding to work out which items you could buy with a £10 note? Which item or items would give the least amount of change?

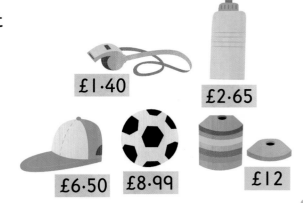

£1·40　£2·65　£6·50　£8·99　£12

# Exploring patterns in the times tables

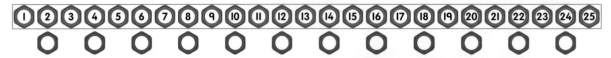

I've used red pegs for the multiples of 1 and blue pegs for the multiples of 2.

## Practice

1 Can you copy and complete this Venn diagram for numbers up to 60?

2 How would you label the group in the middle? What have you found out about these numbers?

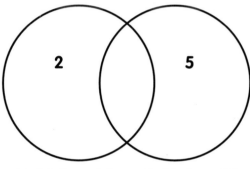

Multiples of 2     Multiples of 5

## Going deeper

This table shows how often trams stop. Each tram starts at the depot, which is stop 0. There are 100 tram stops.

1 Can you work out which stops from 1 to 100 both these trams will stop at?

   a Trams 5 and 10      b Trams 2 and 4

   c Trams 3 and 6

   d Can you explain how you know?

| Tram | Stops |
|------|-------|
| 2 | Every 2 stops |
| 3 | Every 3 stops |
| 4 | Every 4 stops |
| 5 | Every 5 stops |
| 6 | Every 6 stops |
| 7 | Every 7 stops |
| 8 | Every 8 stops |
| 10 | Every 10 stops |

# Number lines and the 2 times table

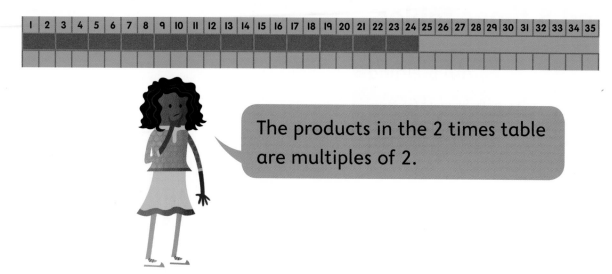

The products in the 2 times table are multiples of 2.

## Practice

1 Can you record the first 10 multiples of 2, starting with 0?

2 These number lines show multiples of 2. Can you copy and complete them? Try writing a multiplying sentence for each missing number.

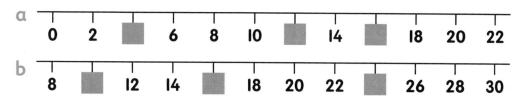

a 0  2  ▢  6  8  10  ▢  14  ▢  18  20  22

b 8  ▢  12  14  ▢  18  20  22  ▢  26  28  30

## Going deeper

1 Can you count in groups to reach these products?
How many ways can you find to reach each number?

   a 24          b 30          c 42          d 50

2 Can you explain how you know you have found all the possible ways in **question 1**?

# Exploring relationships between the 2, 4 and 8 times tables

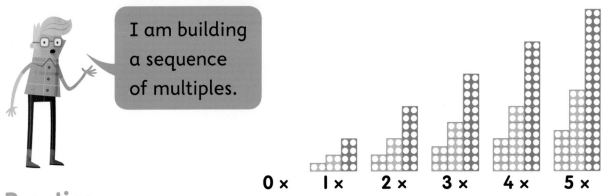

I am building a sequence of multiples.

0 ×  1 ×  2 ×  3 ×  4 ×  5 ×

## Practice

1 Can you copy and complete these sequences of multiples?

  a 2, 4, 6, ▨, 10, 12, ▨, 16, 18, ▨, ▨, 24

  b 4, 8, ▨, 16, 20, ▨, 28, 32, ▨, ▨, 44, ▨

  c What do you notice? Talk about the patterns together.

2 Now can you copy and complete this sequence?

  8, 16, ▨, 32, 40, ▨, 56, 64, 72, ▨, ▨, 96

## Going deeper

1 Can you copy and complete these double multiplying facts?

  a If 3 × 2 = 6, then 3 × 4 = ▨.

  b If 7 × 2 = 14, then 7 × ▨ = 28.

  c If ▨ × 2 = 12, then 6 × 4 = ▨.

  d If ▨ × 4 = 20, then ▨ × 8 = 40.

2 Can you find more pairs of double multiplying facts in the 2, 4 and 8 times tables?

# Using times tables

## Practice

Can you answer questions 1 to 3 and record the multiplying sentence that goes with each one?

1 Each child has a pair of gloves. How many gloves are there?

2 Imran has 8 bags of marbles. There are 5 marbles in each bag. How many marbles does Imran have?

3 Amy puts 10p in her money box each day. She wants to save 70p for a balloon. How many days will it take her?

## Going deeper

1 Can you explain how knowing the 4 times table can help you with other times tables facts?

2 Together, investigate other times tables. Can you find any more that are connected? How do you know?

Explorer Progress Book 3b, pages 20–23

# Exploring sharing and dividing

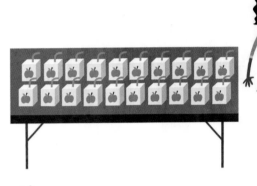

My cousins are coming to stay. I have 20 drinks for them.

## Practice

1 Tia has 4 cousins and they each need 5 drinks. Does she have enough drinks?

2 Can you copy and complete this table?

| Number of children | Number of drinks each | Multiplying sentence |
|---|---|---|
| 4 | 2 | |
| 4 | | 4 × 3 = |
| | | 4 × 4 = 16 |

## Going deeper

1 Look at your completed table for question 2. Can you write a dividing sentence for each multiplying sentence?

2 If 132 ÷ 11 = 12, what is 11 × 12? Can you explain?

3 Is 12 ÷ 3 the same as 3 ÷ 12? Can you explain?

# Using the language of sharing

I have 2 friends visiting and 15 crackers.

I can write how many crackers we will each get as 15 ÷ 3 = ▮.

## Practice

1 How many crackers will Molly and her friends get each?
Can you copy and complete the dividing sentence?

2 Talk about these sharing problems. Can you record the dividing sentences for each?

  a Molly and her 3 friends share out 16 biscuits equally. How many biscuits do they get each?

  b Some friends share 18 sandwiches equally. They get 3 each. How many friends are there?

  c 18 carrot sticks are shared equally between 6 friends. How many carrot sticks can they each have?

## Going deeper

1 Can you write the calculation for each of the Practice questions with both the ÷ and the ⟋‾ symbols? Talk about and record your answers.

2 a Can you write some similar sharing problems? Ask your partner to record the dividing sentences and calculations.

  b Can you find a way to check your partner's answer?

# Using arrays

What is an array? How can it help with dividing and multiplying?

## Practice

1 How would you explain the array above to Ravi?

2 a Can you use 15 counters to make an array? How many different arrays can you make? Record the multiplying sentences for each one.

b Can you write the dividing sentences for each array?

c Now write the number trio for each array.

3 Can you repeat question 2 for the following numbers of counters?

   a 12        b 18        c 24

## Going deeper

1 Can you use arrays to work out the answers to these?

a Lois shares 30 football cards equally between herself and 5 friends. How many cards will they each have?

b Amman has made 42 cupcakes. A box holds 6 cupcakes. How many boxes can he fill?

2 Can you make up some word problems that use dividing? Ask your partner to draw the arrays and write the dividing sentences to find the answer.

# Finding remainders

23 ÷ 10 =

What is a remainder?

## Practice

1 Can you explain to Ben what a remainder is? You can use the Numicon Shapes and example above.

2 Can you record the dividing facts and find the answers to these problems?

 a I have 12 marbles and 5 bags. How many marbles can I put in each bag if I share them out equally?

 b There are 37 books to be shared equally between 6 book boxes. How many books will there be in each box?

 c I bought 27 bananas. They come in bags of 8 or individually. How many bags and how many single bananas did I buy?

## Going deeper

1 Can you find the missing numbers in each of these calculations? Explain how you know.

 a 32 ÷ ▢ = 5 r2  b ▢ ÷ 6 = 3 r1  c 65 ÷ 10 = ▢

2 Can you write a dividing problem to go with each of the calculations in **question 1**?

# Extending sequences

I'm building a sequence of consecutive odd numbers.

1   3   5   7   9

## Practice

1   What do you think the 7th term in Tia's sequence will be?

2   Talk about ways you can record Tia's number sequence. Can you choose a way and record the sequence up to 21?

3   Explore other sequences of odd numbers, starting with 3, then 5 and so on. Can you find the 7th term each time? What do you notice?

## Going deeper

I'm making new sequences of consecutive odd numbers. This time the numbers are decreasing.

9   7   5   3   1

1   If Tia begins with 17, what is the 7th term? How do you know?

2   Tia now starts with the number 27. The 10th term is 9. What are the first ten numbers in her sequence?

# Following rules to extend sequences

I'm trying to find the rule for this sequence of numbers.

1   4   7   10   13

## Practice

1 Can you find the rule for Molly's sequence of Numicon Shapes?

2 Jin uses this rule to make a sequence. Can you record the first 10 terms?

Multiples of 5 plus 2

3 a Can you find a rule for this new sequence?

5, 9, 13, 17, 21, 25

  b What would the 10th term be? How do you know?

## Going deeper

 1 a Can you work out the rule for this sequence together?

1, 6, 11, 16, 21, 26, 31

  b Which of these numbers will be in the sequence if you extend it? Can you explain how you know?

36, 51, 73, 96, 83, 101, 65

2 Can you make up your own sequences? Challenge your partner to find the rules.

# Sequences with decreasing patterns

This is a decreasing pattern.

15    11    7    3

## Practice

1  What is the rule for Ben's sequence?

2  Can you find the rules for these sequences?

   a  35, 30, 25, 20, 15, 10, 5        b  41, 36, 31, 26, 21, 16, 11

   c  151, 146, 141, 136, 131, 126, 121

3  Can you extend these sequences to find the 10th term?

   a  36, 33, 30, 27, ...              b  51, 49, 47, 45, 43, ...

4  Can you explain the rule for each sequence in question 3?

## Going deeper

1  Can you find the 5 missing terms in each of these sequences?
   Explain how you know.

   a  ▢, ▢, ▢, ▢, ▢, 43, 41, 39, 37, 35, 33

   b  ▢, ▢, ▢, ▢, ▢, 26, 24, 22, 20, 18

2  Can you make your own decreasing sequences? Challenge
   your partner to find the rule.

# Finding missing numbers in sequences

Ravi is finding missing numbers in sequences.

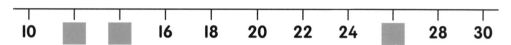

## Practice

1 Can you find the missing numbers in Ravi's sequence?

2 Can you work out the rule for each of these sequences and write down the missing terms?

> Looking at the difference between two numbers in a sequence often helps me to find the rule.

a ▨, 22, 25, 28, ▨, 34, 37

b ▨, 90, ▨, ▨, 75, 70, ▨

c 190, 185, ▨, 175, 170, ▨, 160

d ▨, ▨, 122, 125, ▨, 131, 134, ▨

3 How does knowing the rule help you to find missing terms?

## Going deeper

1 a Can you make your own sequences with missing numbers? Ask your partner to find the rule and fill in the gaps.

  b Talk about and compare your strategies.

2 Can you write a hint for someone who is struggling to find the missing numbers in a sequence?

# Adding and subtracting multiples of 10 and 100

Rob and Marta have these amounts in their money boxes.

Rob  Marta

£8·25  £9·80

## Practice

1 a Marta gives Rob 50p. How much do they each have now?

  b Then they both spend 20p. How much do they each have left?

2 Can you work out these calculations?

  a 35 + 40      b 96 – 60      c 242 + 30

  d 125 + 70     e 532 – 20     f 475 – 40

 3 Can you explain how you worked out your answers to question 2?

## Going deeper

1 a Rob has £8·25. Then he saves 10p a day for one week. How much does he have in total?

  b Marta has £9·80. She spends 10p a day for one week. How much does she have left?

2 a Anton has £5·50 and adds 20p each day. What happens on the 3rd day? Can you explain?

  b Zena has £6·85 and spends 20p each day. How many days will it take for her to have less than £6?

# Adding and subtracting mentally

23          34

I'm working out 23 + 34 using Numicon Shapes.

## Practice

 1 a Can you explain how to work out the total of 23 and 34?

  b Can you work out 34 − 23? Explain your strategy.

2 a What is double 23?

  b What is double 34? How could you show this?

3 Can you solve these?

  a 87 − 14      b 127 + 32      c Double 42      d 146 − 25

.......................................................................................................

## Going deeper

1 a Can you find another pair of numbers with the same total as 23 + 34?

  b How about another?

  c Can you find a pair of numbers that have the same difference as 34 − 23?

  d How about another?

2 For each of your calculations in **question 1**, can you write three other adding and subtracting facts that use the same numbers?

# Crossing 10s and 100s when adding

|  | Class 1 | Class 2 |
|---|---|---|
| Year R | 25 | 26 |
| Year 1 | 28 | 31 |
| Year 2 | 29 | 29 |

## Practice

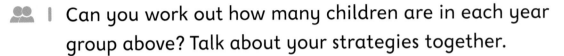

1 Can you work out how many children are in each year group above? Talk about your strategies together.

2 In Year 1, 18 children are boys. How many are girls?

3 How many children are in Year R, 1 and 2 altogether?

4 In another school, there are 117 boys and 125 girls. How many children are there altogether?

...................................................................................................

## Going deeper

1 Can you copy this table and fill in the missing numbers? There must be at least 25 children in each class, and no more than 32.

|  | Class 1 | Class 2 | Class 3 | Total |
|---|---|---|---|---|
| Year R |  |  |  | 81 |
| Year 1 |  |  |  | 95 |
| Year 2 |  |  |  | 88 |

2 Take it in turns to spin a 0 to 9 spinner four times to make a calculation. Can you arrange the digits to give you the largest total?

☐☐ + ☐☐ =

# Subtracting when crossing 10s

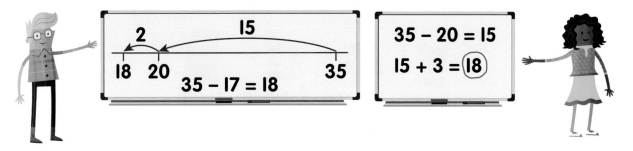

2    15

18   20          35

35 – 17 = 18

35 – 20 = 15

15 + 3 = (18)

## Practice

1 Can you explain both Ben and Tia's strategies for solving 35 – 17?

2 Can you find two different ways to solve 87 – 62? (Your strategies don't have to be the same as Ben and Tia's.) Compare with your partner.

3 Can you solve these?

    a 82 – 28       b 64 – 19       c 55 – 26       d 43 – 37

4 Now solve the calculations in question 3 using a **different** strategy. Talk about your methods with your partner.

## Going deeper

1 Can you explain Tia's strategy using apparatus?

2 Can you write two related subtracting calculations, both with an answer of 15?

3 Look at the calculations in question 3 without looking at your answers. Can you give an equivalent calculation for each one?

For example, 72 – 18 = 74 – 20.

# Exploring Roman numerals

## Practice

1 These children are holding numbers in Roman numerals. Can you write down their numbers in order, smallest first?

2 A clock has Roman numerals. What time does the clock show for each of these?

   a Long hand points to XII, short hand points to IV.

   b Long hand points to VI, short hand points between VII and VIII.

   c Long hand points to XI, short hand points just before IX.

## Going deeper

1 Oscar has four Roman numeral cards and one adding symbol.

   a He arranges the cards to show VI + IX. How many other additions can you find that use all the cards?

   b Now can you give the answers to each addition in Roman numerals?

# Telling the time on a 12-hour digital clock

| Times in the morning | Times in the afternoon |
|---|---|
|  |  |

## Practice

1 These are some of the clocks in Ravi's house. What might Ravi be doing at each of these times, if it is a normal school day?

**GMS 3** 2 Can you draw the above times on a blank clock face?

## Going deeper

**GMS 3** 1 What events happen in your usual school day before 1 o'clock in the afternoon? For example: assembly, break, lunch. Choose five and find out what time each happens.

a Draw these times on a blank clock face.

b Can you write the digital time below each one?

2 Write down six digital clock times each on pieces of paper. Choose times that are in the morning between 6 o'clock and 12 o'clock.

a Ask your partner to put your times in order as quickly as they can. Do the same with your partner's times.

b Now mix up the times. Can you work together to put all your 12 times in order as quickly as you can?

# Telling the time to the nearest minute

## Practice

1 What times do these clocks show?

a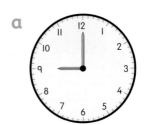

b

c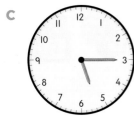

d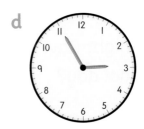

e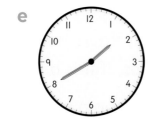

f

2 Can you draw each time below on a blank clock face?

a 4:20　　b 6:45　　c 9:00　　d 9:05　　e 9:04

················································································

## Going deeper

1 Can you make a list of any times that are the same?

| | | | |
|---|---|---|---|
| 4:15 | 2:15 | quarter to two | 3:10 |
| ten past three |  | 2:45 | 1:45 |
|  | quarter to one | quarter past two |  |

# Solving problems with time

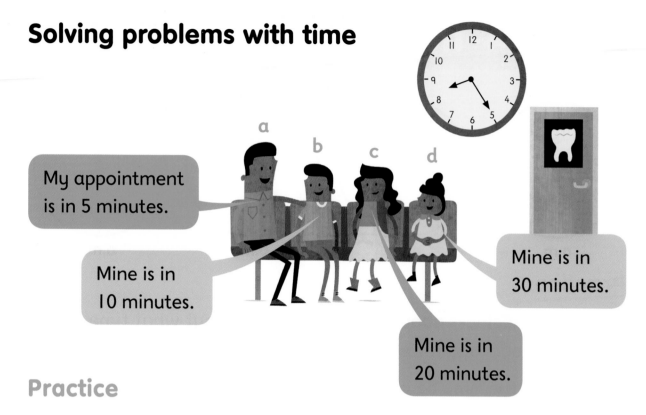

## Practice

1  The Crown family are at the dentist. What time will each person go in?

2  It is 3:50 in the afternoon. Ella left school 20 minutes ago, Ali left 40 minutes ago, and Holly left a quarter of an hour ago. What time did they each leave school?

## Going deeper

1  At 10:55 in the morning, Dan is watching a race he filmed. The runners were Lilly, Seth, Dipa and Otto. Lilly finished 10 minutes ago and Seth finished 4 minutes after Lilly. Dipa finished 25 minutes earlier than Lilly and Otto finished half an hour ago.

Can you work out who won the race, and what time each runner finished?

# The 24-hour day

a.m.          p.m.          p.m.          a.m.

## Practice

1 Look at the clocks above. Can you work out out what time it was 5 hours ago for each clock? Will it be a.m. or p.m.?

2 What will the time be on each clock in 4 hours' time?

................................................................................................

## Going deeper

1 I need to arrive at 1:15 p.m. and my journey takes $2\frac{1}{2}$ hours. When should I leave?

2 Kareem needs 8 hours' sleep. If he goes to bed at 8:45 p.m., what time should he set his alarm for in the morning?

3 It takes 25 minutes to make a pie and 2 hours for it to cook in the oven. If the pie needs to be ready for 1:00 p.m., when should you start making it?

4 Yesterday Anna ran a marathon. She started at 9:30 a.m. and finished at 2:00 p.m. How long did it take Anna to run the race?

# Exploring seconds, minutes, hours, days and weeks

## Practice

1 Can you copy and complete these sentences?

a There are _____ seconds in a minute.

b There are _____ minutes in an hour.

c There are _____ hours in a day.

d There are _____ days in a week.

e There are just over _____ weeks in a month.

f There are _____ months in a year.

## Going deeper

1 Some of these cards show the same amount of time. How many matching cards can you find? Write down all the matches you find.

2 Take turns to choose an amount of time. Can you give this time in a different way? How many different ways can you find?

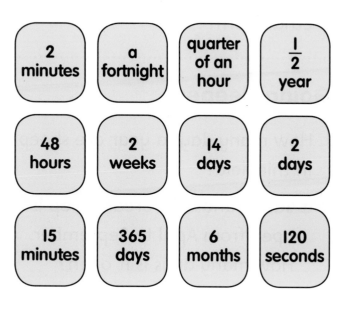

# Exploring the number of days and months in a year

Roadworks
expected
from
March 2018
to
May 2020.

## Practice

1  For how many months are the roadworks expected to last?

2  Mrs Romaine is going on a cruise that lasts for all of July and August. For how many days will she be away?

3  Ethan's age is 8 years 3 months. How many months ago was Ethan born?

## Going deeper

Sheep are only allowed in this field between October and March.

1  How many days a year are sheep allowed in this field?

2  a  Salty Sands Ice Cream shop is only open from April to September. How many days is it open?

   b  Can you now work out how many days it is closed?

# Exploring years, decades, centuries and millennia

millennium

century ▬

decade ▮

year |

## Practice

**1** Can you copy and complete these sentences?

a There are _____ years in a decade.

b There are _____ years in a century.

c There are _____ decades in a century.

d There are _____ centuries in a millennium.

e There are _____ years in a millennium.

f There are _____ years in 2 decades.

g There are _____ years in 3 centuries.

h There are _____ years in 4 millennia.

## Going deeper

**1** In which century were you born? Were you born in the same century as your parents or guardian? If not, in which century were they born?

**2** How about your grandparents or oldest family member? In which century were they born?

**3** If a cricket player gets a 'double century', how many runs do you think they have scored?

# Adding using grouping and regrouping

Ravi and Molly take a large handful of straws each and count them by grouping in tens.

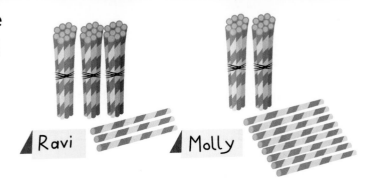

## Practice

1  a  Can you use straws or base-ten apparatus to show how many straws Molly and Ravi have altogether?

   b  How could you record your practical work using a column written method?

2  Each take a big handful of straws (or counters).

   a  Estimate how many you have. Then count by grouping in tens.

   b  What is the total of both your sets?

   c  Record your work using a column written method.

## Going deeper

1  Ravi and Molly add a further 80 straws to their combined pile. How many straws will they have? Write the calculation.

2  Can you make up your own calculation that requires:

   a  regrouping once        b  regrouping twice?

# Adding hundreds, tens and ones

Ben and Tia take turns to pick two numbers on the board and add them together. If the total is on the board, they cover the total with a counter. Ben is red and Tia is blue.

| 130 | 131 | 132 | 133 | 134 | 135 | 136 | 137 | 138 | 139 |
| 250 | 251 | 252 | 253 | 254 | 255 | 256 | 257 | 258 | 259 |
| 320 | 321 | 322 | 323 | 324 | 325 | 326 | 327 | 328 | 329 |
| 440 | 441 | 442 | 443 | 444 | 445 | 446 | 447 | 448 | 449 |
| 515 | 516 | 517 | 518 | 519 | 520 | 521 | 522 | 523 | 524 |
| 560 | 561 | 562 | 563 | 537 | 538 | 539 | 540 | 541 | 569 |
| 610 | 611 | 612 | 613 | 614 | 615 | 616 | 617 | 618 | 619 |
| ● | 781 | 782 | 783 | 784 | 785 | 786 | 787 | 788 | 789 |
| 870 | ● | 872 | 873 | 874 | 875 | 876 | 877 | 878 | 879 |
| 990 | 991 | 992 | 993 | 994 | 995 | 996 | 997 | 998 | 999 |

## Practice

1 Ben picks 254 and 617. Tia picks 522 and 258. What numbers must be covered by the red and blue counters? How can you check they have calculated their total correctly?

 2 Try the game. Before you choose your two numbers, estimate to make sure their total will not be more than 999. Play until you have each covered four squares.

## Going deeper

1 How could you make the total 517 using the numbers in the square?

2 Ben chooses one number that is greater than 500 and one that is less than 300. The total of his two numbers is a multiple of 5. What could his two numbers be? List three possibilities.

# Adding using an abacus

Molly makes her own abacus using counters and a HTO frame and Tia makes hers using cubes.

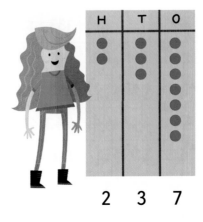

2  3  7

4  7  9

## Practice

1  If Molly and Tia add 134 to each of their numbers, what will their new numbers be?

2  If Molly and Tia add their new numbers together, what will their total be?

3  Make your own abacus using apparatus of your choice. Can you show the total of 123 + 32 + 241?

4  Can you show 235 + 132 + 116? Explain what you did and then record this using a written column method.

## Going deeper

1  a  What does Molly need to add to her abacus in the picture above to make the number 712?

   b  What does Tia need to add to hers to make the number 923?

2  a  Discuss how you might add another 247 to 923. Think about how the abacus could help you.

   b  Can you explain how regrouping works for adding any numbers together?

# Deciding when to use the column method for adding

## Practice

1 Can you explain why the calculations have been put into each section?

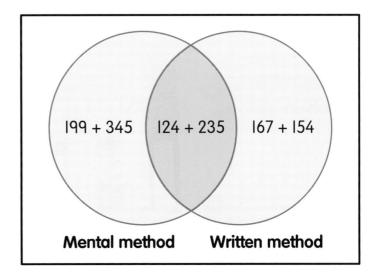

199 + 345    124 + 235    167 + 154

Mental method    Written method

2 a Copy the Venn diagram. Can you put the calculations below into your diagram to show how you would solve each one?

56 + 48    103 + 78    132 + 58    £5·80 + £2·20    56p + 28p + 67p

432 + 521    258 + 379    £1·55 + 78p + £1·65    397 + 253

  b Now solve the calculations. Estimate the answer first.

  c Compare your Venn diagrams. Did you make the same choices?

## Going deeper

1 Can you copy and complete these calculations? You also need to show where the carried digits should be.

a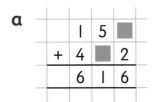

b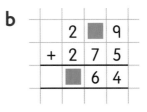

# Solving subtraction problems to 100

My sunflower is 68 cm tall.

My sunflower is 54 cm tall.

## Practice

1  a How many more centimetres does Ben's sunflower need to grow to reach 1 m in height?

   b How many more centimetres does Molly's sunflower need to grow to reach 1 m?

   c How much taller is Ben's sunflower than Molly's?

2 Ben and Molly each have a jug of 100 ml of water.

   Molly adds 35 ml to her flower pot. Ben adds 46 ml to his flower pot. How much is left in each of their jugs?

## Going deeper

1 Can you model two **different** ways to show 100 − 68 on a number line or number rod track?

2 Ben's sunflower grows a further 7 cm in a week.

   How can you use your answer to question 1 a to work out how much more it needs to grow to reach 1 m?

# Subtracting by mentally counting on

I've used 55 g of flour.

I've used 38 g of sugar.

## Practice

1 When Tia started baking, there was 82 g of flour in the bag. How much flour is left in the bag now?

2 When Ravi started baking, there was 152 g of sugar in the bag. How much sugar is left in the bag now?

3 Can you solve these calculations?

    a 86 – 68         b 122 – 118         c 164 – 145

 4 Compare your methods for question 3 with your partner.

## Going deeper

1 Can you solve these in three jumps or fewer on a number line?

    a 76 – 48               b 172 – 139

   c Compare your jumps with your partner.

 2 a What could the subtracting calculation be for this number line?

b Can you suggest a **different** calculation it could be?

# Deciding when to use a written method

I think 874 – 631 is easier
to solve than 71 – 42.

## Practice

1 Can you explain why Molly might think this?

2 Can you write three subtracting calculations you can do
   mentally, then solve them?

3 Now write three subtracting calculations you don't think
   you can do mentally. Discuss with your partner why not.

4 Can you solve these? Check with the inverse calculation.

   a  96 – 23              b  467 – 234              c  184 – 121

## Going deeper

1 Talk about how you could solve both of Molly's calculations.

2 Angus has made 546 with these cards.
   What 3-digit numbers could he subtract to give
   him an answer between 305 and 320?
   Give three possible numbers, each with a different
   digit in the tens column.

   5  4  6

3 Take it in turns to turn over three number cards to make
   a 3-digit number. Can you subtract another 3-digit number
   to give you a difference less than 100?

# The column method for subtracting

Amir is solving 875 – 358. He makes the number 875 on a place value frame but is stuck on the next step.

| Hundreds | Tens | Ones |
|----------|------|------|
| 800 | 70 | 5 |

## Practice

1 a Can you explain how to solve this calculation?

   b Why is this harder than 875 – 652?

2 Can you solve these?

   a 364 – 147          b 764 – 216          c 538 – 265

## Going deeper

1 What other subtracting calculations starting with 875 is Amir likely to get stuck on for the same reasons? Can you list three?

2 Can you work out the missing numbers in the calculations below? Explain to your partner how you worked them out.

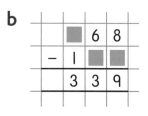

a
```
    5 ■ ■
-   2 3 5
    3 2 7
```

b
```
    ■ 6 8
-   1 ■ ■
    3 3 9
```

# How many times bigger?

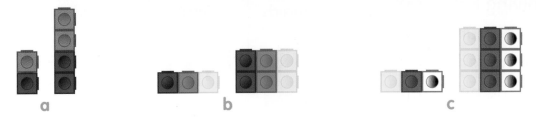

a          b          c

## Practice

1  For each pair of cube patterns, say how many times bigger one is than the other. Can you record a multiplying sentence for each set?

2  Can you multiply this cube pattern by 2 and then by 3? Write the multiplying sentences.

3  Can you make or draw cube patterns for these pairs of multiplying facts?

   a  3 × 1 and 3 × 3     b  4 × 1 and 4 × 2     c  3 × 2 and 4 × 2

## Going deeper

1  There are some gaps in this cupcake recipe for 1, 2 and 6 people. Can you write down the missing amounts for each letter?

| Ingredients | Serves 1 | Serves 2 | Serves 6 |
|---|---|---|---|
| 3 eggs | 3 | 6 | a |
| 1 cup of flour | 1 | b | c |
| 10 ml milk | 10 ml | d | e |
| 5 spoons of sugar | f | 10 | g |

2  What if you needed to make this recipe for 5 people? How could you work this out quickly?

# How many times smaller? How many times longer?

## Practice

1 Look at this pattern. Can you draw the pattern that is half the size? Can you record the dividing sentence?

2 Now look at this pattern. Can you draw the pattern that is three times as long? Can you record the multiplying sentence?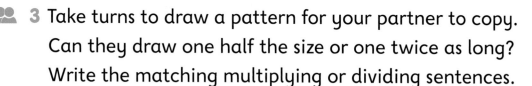

3 Take turns to draw a pattern for your partner to copy. Can they draw one half the size or one twice as long? Write the matching multiplying or dividing sentences.

## Going deeper

Ray is making bracelets with beads. This is his pattern.

1 How many beads would be needed for a bracelet:

  a twice as long    b four times as long    c ten times as long?

2 Design a bracelet pattern by drawing coloured beads.

  a Can your partner use your pattern to show a bracelet 2, 3, 4, 5 or 10 times longer?

  b Can your partner use your pattern to show a bracelet half the size or three times smaller?

3 Can you find two different ways to describe the relationships between:

  a the blue and the light green number rods

  b the brown and the red number rods?

# Finding rules for multiplying and dividing by 10

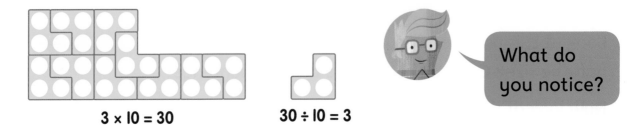

$3 \times 10 = 30$ $\qquad$ $30 \div 10 = 3$

What do you notice?

## Practice

1 a Can you copy and compete these multiplying facts?

$1 \times \blacksquare = 10$ $\qquad$ $\blacksquare \times 10 = 50$ $\qquad$ $2 \times 10 = \blacksquare$

$6 \times \blacksquare = 60$ $\qquad$ $\blacksquare \times 10 = 30$ $\qquad$ $7 \times 10 = \blacksquare$

b How do you know that you have the right numbers?

2 a Can you copy and complete these dividing facts?

$10 \div 10 = \blacksquare$ $\qquad$ $50 \div 10 = \blacksquare$ $\qquad$ $\blacksquare \div 10 = 2$

$\blacksquare \div 10 = 6$ $\qquad$ $30 \div \blacksquare = 3$ $\qquad$ $\blacksquare \div 10 = 7$

b Explain how you know that you have the right answers.

## Going deeper

1 a Can you make these numbers 10 times bigger?  10, 6, 12, 7, 9, 1

  b Can you make these numbers 10 times smaller?  80, 50, 110, 20, 30, 40

  c Can you explain how you worked these out?

2 How many other multiplying and dividing facts can you find that go together?

# Short written methods for multiplying and dividing

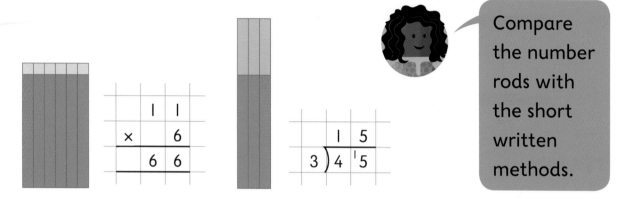

Compare the number rods with the short written methods.

## Practice

Can you use a short written method to answer these?

1  15 children are making muffins. How many muffins will there be if each child makes:

a 5            b 3            c 6            d 9?

2  12 children made the same number of muffins each. If there are this many muffins, how many did each child make?

a 120          b 24           c 132          d 96

..............................................................................................

## Going deeper

1 a Lyle has 110 football cards and wants to put them into packs of 10. How many packs can he make?

b What if Lyle wants to put his 110 cards into packs of 5?

2 a Jessica has 7 packs of football cards, with 12 in each pack. How many cards does she have in total?

b How many cards will she have if she gets 2 more packs?

# Exploring perimeters

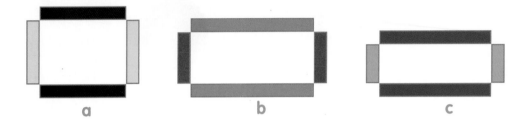

a          b          c

## Practice

1 Use number rods to make each of the rectangles. Can you find the perimeter of each rectangle, using the rods and a number rod track or 30 cm ruler?

2 Now can you draw the rectangles in your maths book? Use a ruler to make the sides the correct length.

.....................................................................................

## Going deeper

1 Tia has made these three shapes from rods. Can you help her to work out the perimeter of each shape?

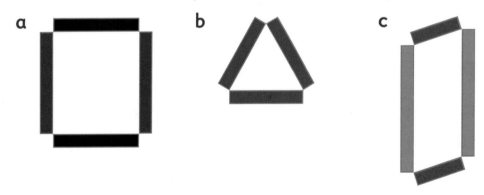

a          b          c

2 Using number rods, how many rectangles can you make with a perimeter of 20 cm?

# Exploring millimetres, centimetres and metres

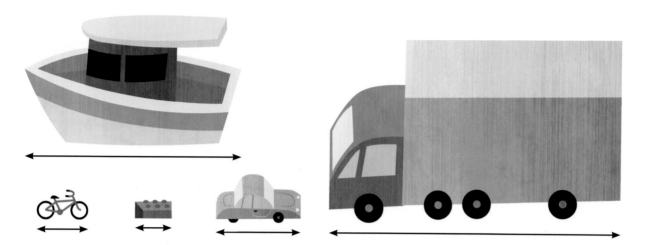

## Practice

1 Measure the length of each toy in millimetres with a ruler. Can you put the toys in order of size, starting with the smallest?

2 A worm is 4 cm 5 mm long. What is its length in millimetres?

3 The wingspan of an eagle is 1 m 52 cm. How long would this be if it was measured in centimetres?

............................................................................................................

## Going deeper

1 Roll a dice to get a length in centimetres. Roll again for a length in millimetres. Add these together and draw a line of that length. Can you repeat this five times and label each line in millimetres?

2 A toy train engine is 6 cm long. Each carriage is 74 mm long.

   a How long is the train engine with two carriages?

   b What length is the engine with four carriages?

# Calculating with lengths

## Practice

The gap is 1 m wide.

1  Nina is putting a 600 mm kitchen unit into the gap. How wide is the gap that will be left? Give your answer in centimetres and also in millimetres.

2  Dory makes this picture frame. The dark pieces of wood are 80 mm long and 10 mm wide. The light pieces of wood are 120 mm long and 10 mm wide. How tall will it be? How wide will it be?

........................................................................

## Going deeper

1  Look at question 2. Dory is using the same sized wood for this new frame design. How tall and wide will the frame be now?

2  a Dory puts a photo in each frame. They fit exactly. What are their dimensions in millimetres?

   b Can you also answer in centimetres?

# Collecting and presenting data

Ravi     Tia     Molly     Ben

## Practice

1 Ravi, Tia, Molly and Ben have borrowed some books from the library. Can you copy and complete this tally chart to show this data?

| Name | Tally |
|------|-------|
| Ravi | |
| Tia | |
| Molly | |
| Ben | |

2 Can you draw a pictogram to display the data? Use a circle to represent two books.

## Going deeper

This pictogram shows the number of socks the children find under their beds.

| Name | Socks |
|------|-------|
| Ravi | ⌇ ⌇ ⌇ ⌇ |
| Tia | ⌇ ⌇ |
| Molly | ⌇ ⌇ ⌇ |
| Ben | ⌇ ⌇ ⌇ ⌇ ⌇ ⌇ |

1 a They find 60 socks altogether. How many socks does each symbol represent?

b Can you work out how many socks each child found?

# Finding amounts and paying in coins

Bat £1·10    Shorts £3·15    T-shirt £2·55    Water  80p

## Practice

1 For each purse, what item can you buy using all the coins?

a  10p 10p 50p 10p

b  £2 20p 20p 10p 5p

c  50p 20p 20p 20p

2 How would you make the following amounts of money using the fewest coins?

a 19p          b £1·30          c 34p          d 95p          e 77p

## Going deeper

1 a Chris has 4 coins in his pocket that total 50p. What could the coins be?

b Kim has 6 coins that total £1. What could the coins be?

2 How many ways could you buy 2 different pieces of fruit, using exactly 6 coins?

25p

30p    43p

# Receiving change

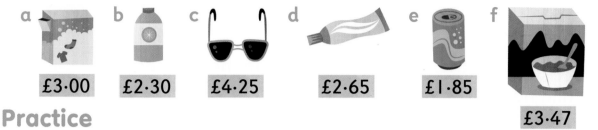

a £3·00  b £2·30  c £4·25  d £2·65  e £1·85  f £3·47

## Practice

1 Amanda has a £5 note. For each item above, how much change would she get?

2 Jerry has a £10 note. How much change would he get if he bought these from the items shown above:

a 2 pairs of sunglasses

b 1 bottle of juice and 1 packet of cereal

c 2 cans of drink

d 1 tube of toothpaste and 1 box of soap powder?

## Going deeper

1 The children each use a £10 note to buy 2 items from this list. Can you explain who bought what and how you know?

| scissors £3·45 | pen £3·00 | envelopes £3·47 | paperclips £2·65 | glue £2·30 | ruler £1·85 |
|---|---|---|---|---|---|

Ravi: I got £4·25 change.

Molly: I got £4·35 change.

Tia: I got £3·53 change.

Ben: I got £5·85 change.

# Adjusting and totaling money amounts

## Practice

1 After buying their treats, how much money will each child have left?

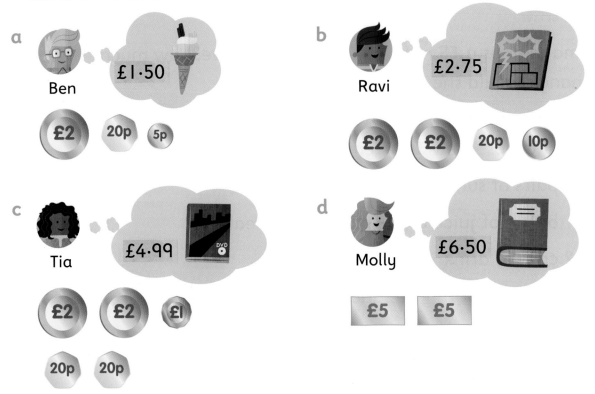

a  Ben  £1·50
£2  20p  5p

b  Ravi  £2·75
£2  £2  20p  10p

c  Tia  £4·99
£2  £2  £1
20p  20p

d  Molly  £6·50
£5  £5

## Going deeper

1 How could you pay for each of these drinks exactly using the smallest number of coins?

a Sparkling Spritz £2·40    b Fruit Fizz £3·15
c Banana Shake £3·20    d Strawberry Smoothie £2·99

2 If you bought one of each of the drinks above, how much change would you get from a £20 note?

# Buying multiple items and working out the savings

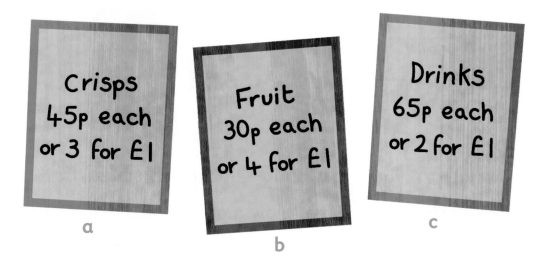

Crisps
45p each
or 3 for £1

a

Fruit
30p each
or 4 for £1

b

Drinks
65p each
or 2 for £1

c

## Practice

1 If you spend £1 on each of the three multipack offers above, how much money will you save on each offer?

2 Ben would like 6 action figures for his birthday. They cost £1·50 each. He is given a £20 note. If he uses the money to buy all 6 action figures, how much change will he get?

## Going deeper

1 Rami is given a deal where he can buy 3 items for the price of 2. Rami buys 6 rolls. If a roll costs 50p, how much does Rami save?

2 Sadie invites 12 people to her party. They each get crisps, fruit and a drink. How much does she save by buying the multipacks above?

# Exploring fractions and dividing

## Practice

For each question, write the dividing sentence and a fraction statement.

1 Molly has 6 carrots. How many will each horse get?

2 If Molly only had 3 carrots, how many carrots would each horse get? Explain how you worked out your answer.

3 Another 2 horses arrive. How many carrots will each horse get if Molly has:

    a 8 carrots               b 5 carrots?

........................................................................................

## Going deeper

1 Which will give you more? Sharing 5 between 2 or sharing 9 between 4? Can you explain your reasoning?

2 Carl says you can't halve odd numbers. Why might he think that?

3 a Start at 24. Take turns to halve it (divide it by 2) or quarter it (divide it by 4) until you reach a number between 0 and 2. Can you write your number chain as you say it?

    b Now choose a different starting number that is even and less than 24. What number do you get down to this time?

# Halving numbers

How can I use the pan balance to find a half?

## Practice

1 How can you use the pan balance to solve $\frac{1}{2}$ of 16?

2 Can you solve the following in a similar way?

   a $\frac{1}{2}$ of 28         b $\frac{1}{2}$ of 32         c $\frac{1}{2}$ of 54

3 What is half of 50p? Can you explain how you know?

## Going deeper

1 Jenny is thinking of a whole number. Half her number is greater than 5 but less than 10. Can you list all the numbers Jenny could be thinking of?

2 Put two Numicon Shapes in a feely bag. This is 'half' of a number. Can your partner use questioning to work out what the starting number must be?

3 If this rocket weighs 90 g, what does each brick weigh?

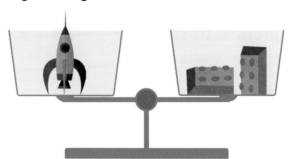

# Finding how many halves

If I eat 4 halves of toast, that is 2 whole slices.

## Practice

1 Can you draw a picture to explain why Tia is correct?

2 How many halves will there be in 4 slices of toast?

3 How many slices of toast does Tia need to make 6 halves?

4 In a small loaf, there are 12 slices of bread. How many halves of toast will this make?

## Going deeper

1 How many pieces of 50 cm string can you cut from 5 m? Can you explain how you worked this out?

2 Here is a pizza that is divided into 6 equal slices. If each slice is halved, how many slices of pizza will there be now?

3 Can you draw a picture to show $\frac{1}{2} + \frac{1}{2} + \frac{1}{2} + \frac{1}{2} + \frac{1}{2} + \frac{1}{2}$?

# Finding quarters

## Practice

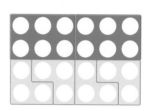

1  What fractions of 12 could Rob be working out using these Numicon Shapes?

2  Can you work out $\frac{1}{4}$ of:

   a  24　　　　　b  40　　　　　c  64?

3  a  How many oranges must Lin have bought if she has 12 quarters?

   b  How many quarters would there be altogether in 8 oranges?

·····································································

## Going deeper

1  a  Can you write clear instructions for how to work out $\frac{1}{4}$ of a number?

   b  Now you want anyone following your instructions to get an answer that is a whole number. Can you explain what the starting number must be and why?

   c  How many $\frac{1}{4}\ell$ cups can you fill from 2 litres?

2  The lucky dip is 25p a go. How many goes could someone have for £5? Can you explain how you know? How does this relate to quarters?

# Using grams and kilograms

## Practice

1 What is the reading on each of these scales?

a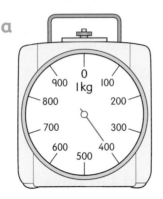

b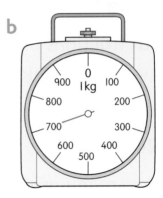

2 What is the mass of each of these bags in kilograms? Can you also write the mass in grams?

a

b

## Going deeper

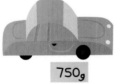

1 What items can you add to make the scales balance? Can you find more than one way to do it?

a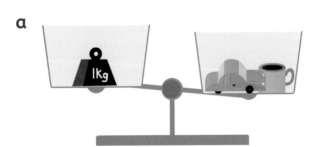

b

# Scaling recipe quantities

Here are the ingredients for vegetable soup.

## Practice

1 How much of each ingredient would you need for 2 people?

2 How much of each for 3 people?

3 If 4 people wanted soup, how much of each ingredient would be needed?

**Vegetable soup**

Serves 1

- 200 g chopped carrots
- 1 tablespoon of oil
- 500 ml stock
- 150 g onions
- 75 g celery

## Going deeper

1 Jay makes these cakes for a party using 15 eggs. How much of each of the other ingredients will he need?

**Cupcakes**

- 250 g butter
- 3 eggs
- 150 g caster sugar
- 100 g self-raising flour
- 2 tablespoons of milk
- 250 g icing sugar

2 This lasagne recipe is for 6 people. Can you rewrite it for 3 people? Now try this for 2 people.

**Lasagne**

- 450 g beef
- 1 onion
- 600 ml sauce
- 150 g cheese
- 12 sheets of lasagne

# Measuring and calculating with grams

## Practice

1 What is the mass of 3 of these bars of chocolate?

2 Ron has 4 candles. If the total mass is 200 g, what is the mass of 1 candle?

3 Maria has 300 g of cereal and Niall has 200 g. Can you say how much cereal they have altogether?

4 A pack of biscuits weighs 500 g. Jim's family eat half the biscuits. What is the mass of the remaining biscuits?

5 Three friends share a 150 g tub of yoghurt equally. Can you say how much they each eat?

100 g

........................................................................................

## Going deeper

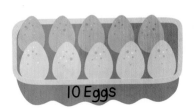

Butter 500 g

Flour 1 kg

10 Eggs

Milk ½ litre

1 Rohan wants to make some cakes but he doesn't want to waste any ingredients. Can you work out how many cakes he could make, and how many of each item he should buy? He wants to use up everything he buys.

**For 1 cake:**
200 g of butter
4 eggs
200 g of flour
100 ml milk

# Money and data handling

20p     25p     30p

## Practice

**1** Can you find the cost of the following items?

    a 3 apples            b 3 bananas

    c 4 pears            d 2 apples and a pear

    e 2 of each item       f 2 apples, 3 pears and 4 bananas

    g 10 apples           h 10 bananas

    i 10 pears

**2** a Between 9 a.m. and 10 a.m. a shop sells 12 apples, 15 bananas and 8 pears. Draw a tally chart to show this.

    b Can you show this data on a bar chart?

## Going deeper

**1** What fruit could you buy above that would cost exactly £1? How many different answers can you find?

**2** Which fruit could you buy for exactly £2? Can you find all the possible answers?

**3** Use the data from your tally chart in question 2. Can you work out how much money the shop gets between 9 a.m. and 10 a.m. from selling these items?

# Reading a scale in millilitres

## Practice

1 How much liquid is in each of these jugs?

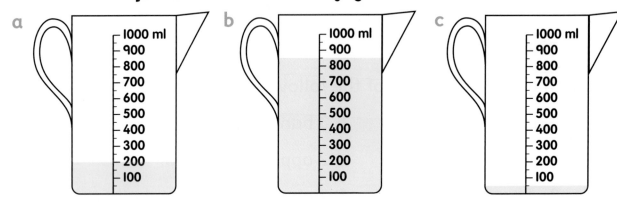

a    b    c

2 Can you match each container to the correct amount?

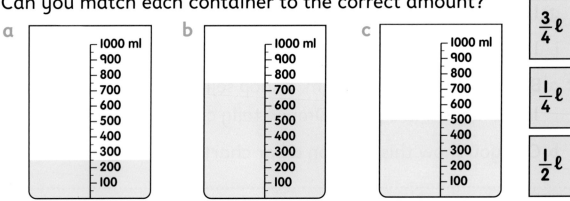

a    b    c

$\frac{3}{4}\ell$

$\frac{1}{4}\ell$

$\frac{1}{2}\ell$

## Going deeper

1 Can you estimate how much liquid is in each of these containers?

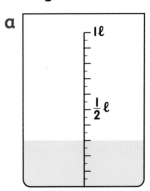

a

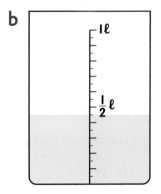

b

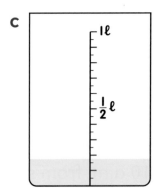

c

# Changing fractions of a litre to millilitres

## Practice

1. a Can you arrange these 12 amounts in size order, starting with the smallest?

   b Now can you match any equivalent amounts?

| | | | |
|---|---|---|---|
| 200 ml | $\frac{1}{4}$ ℓ | $\frac{3}{4}$ ℓ | 600 ml |
| 250 ml | 1 ℓ | $\frac{1}{2}$ ℓ | 350 ml |
| 300 ml | 999 ml | 1000 ml | 0 ml |

........................................................................

## Going deeper

| | 1 ℓ | 250 ml | 500 ml | 740 ml | 400 ml |
|---|---|---|---|---|---|
| Alex's cards: | $\frac{1}{4}$ ℓ | $\frac{1}{2}$ ℓ | 300 ml | 600 ml | $\frac{3}{4}$ ℓ |

Alex is playing a game using these five cards and the chart. He can move the cards and choose which column on the chart he puts each card in.

He compares his cards to the volumes on the chart. He scores 1 point if his card is a larger volume, 0 points if it is smaller and 2 points if it is equal.

1 What is the highest score Alex could get with his cards?

2 What is the lowest score Alex could get with his cards?

3 What other possible scores could Alex get?

# Adding and subtracting volumes of liquid

## Practice

Can you answer these questions?
Explain your workings.

550 ml

1 Kirsty drinks 130 ml. How much juice is left in this carton?

2 Max drinks a 150 ml glass of water, 4 times a day. How much is that altogether?

3 The label on Amir's medicine says, "Take 10 ml, 3 times a day". How much will he take in two days?

4 Jo makes 1 litre of soup but only eats $\frac{1}{4}$ of it. How many millilitres of soup are left?

5 3 bottles of shampoo contain 100 ml, 330 ml and 270 ml each. How much shampoo is that altogether?

....................................................................................................

## Going deeper

1 Arlo has been asked to measure out exactly 2 litres of water, using a 3 ℓ jug and a 5 ℓ jug. He can fill either jug or pour from one jug in to the other. How could Arlo do this?

3 ℓ

5 ℓ

# Mixed units of litres and millilitres

> **Sauce recipe**
> Place chopped vegetables in a large pan.
> Add I litre of water and simmer for 2 hours.
> Then add 200 ml of water before serving.

## Practice

1 If Ross makes two batches of sauce, how much water will he need altogether?

2 Sami drinks a 300 ml milkshake every day. How much milkshake will Sami drink in a week?

3 How many millilitres are there in $1\frac{1}{2}\ell$?

4 A pan holds $2\ell$ 400 ml. How many millilitres is that?

## Going deeper

1 Alva makes I litre of squash for himself and two friends. They each pour a 75 ml glass of squash. How many times can they each do this?

2 A bottle contains 250 ml of medicine. The doctor tells Helen to take 10 ml, 3 times a day. How many days will the medicine last? Can you explain your reasoning?

# Comparing parts with wholes

The children share 12 blocks equally.

My blocks are red.

Mine are yellow.

Mine are green.

Mine are blue.

## Practice

1 What fraction of the blocks does each child have?

2 Ben and Ravi put all their blocks together to make a tower. What fraction of the tower is yellow? What fraction is green?

3 Molly wants to make a new tower and $\frac{1}{3}$ of it should be red. How many children does she need to combine her blocks with?

## Going deeper

The children get a new number of blocks. Ben has 3 green blocks, Molly has 2 red blocks, Tia has 3 blue blocks and Ravi has 4 yellow blocks.

1 Three of the children put their blocks together to make a tower. $\frac{2}{8}$ of the tower is red. Which three children was it?

2 One child goes home, and the rest combine all their blocks to make a tower. Exactly $\frac{1}{3}$ of the tower is blue. Who went home? Can you explain?

# Using fractions to compare parts

Tia: I have £12.

Ravi: I have £8.

Ben: I have £16.

## Practice

1 Molly has half as much money as one of the other children. What is the most she could have? How do you know?

2 One of the children works out that $\frac{1}{4}$ of their money is £3. Who is it?

3 If Ravi saves $\frac{3}{4}$ of his money, and spends the rest, what fraction does he spend? How much money is this?

## Going deeper

1 Which fraction is larger: $\frac{1}{99}$ or $\frac{1}{100}$? Can you explain?

2 Which fraction is larger: $\frac{2}{50}$ or $\frac{2}{60}$? Can you explain?

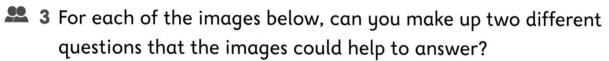 3 For each of the images below, can you make up two different questions that the images could help to answer?

a

b

c

# Exploring fractions as numbers on a number line

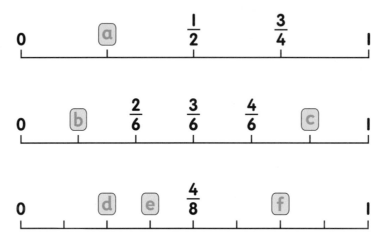

## Practice

| Can you write down the value of each letter on the number lines above?

## Going deeper

| Can you write down the value of each letter on these number lines? You can draw the number lines if it helps you.

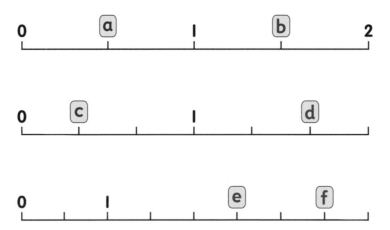

# Exploring equivalence

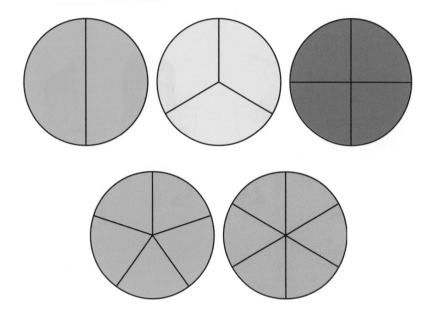

## Practice

1 Using the fraction pieces above, can you find fractions equivalent to:

   a $\frac{1}{2}$          b $\frac{1}{3}$          c $\frac{2}{3}$          d 1?

..................................................................................

## Going deeper

 1 Using only eighths and quarters, how many different combinations can you find that make one whole?

2 If you only use halves, thirds and sixths, how many different combinations can you find to make one whole?

3 If you only use thirds, quarters and fifths, how many different ways can you find to make one whole? Can you explain why this question is different to **questions 1** and **2**?

# Fractions of a set

## Practice

1 a What fraction of the chairs are red?

b What fraction of the cups are empty?

c What fraction of the people are wearing a hat?

d What fraction of the people are not wearing glasses?

2 Can you copy and then colour in $\frac{1}{3}$ of each of these shapes?

a

b

c

## Going deeper

1 a Compare two of these Numicon Shapes at a time. What fractions can you find? Try to find all the possibilities.

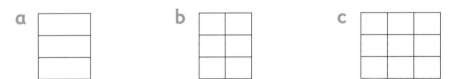

b Can you write each one as a fraction and in words?

# Recognizing fractions

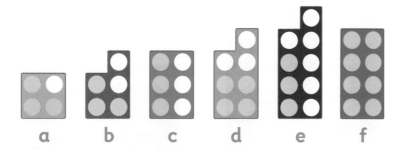

## Practice

1 What fraction of each Numicon Shape is covered by yellow counters?

2 Are any of the fractions shown equal to a half?

3 Are any of the fractions shown equal to a third?

4 What fraction of each Numicon Shape is not covered?

## Going deeper

1 What fraction of each length is red? You can use number rods to help you.

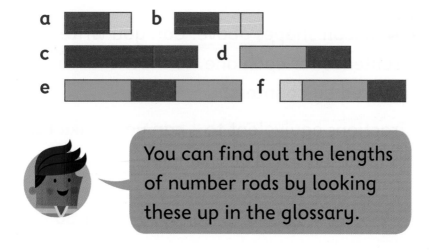

You can find out the lengths of number rods by looking these up in the glossary.

# Adding, subtracting and finding equivalent fractions

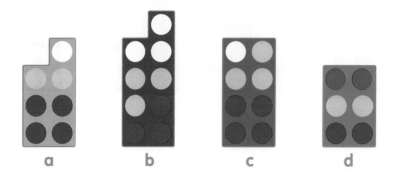

a          b          c          d

## Practice

1  a Look at each of these Numicon Shapes. Can you write the fraction of the whole covered by blue counters?

   b What fraction is covered by yellow counters?

2 Now look at the fraction of each Numicon Shape that is covered by counters altogether. Can you write an adding sentence to show this for each Numicon Shape?

...........................................................................................

## Going deeper

1 Look at the Numicon Shapes above. Can you write a subtracting sentence for each one, to show the fraction that is not covered by counters?

2 How many fractions equivalent to $\frac{1}{2}$ can you make using two numbers from this list? For example, $\frac{10}{20}$.

2, 5, 34, 4, 120, 40, 15, 20, 17, 60, 10, 68, 30

# Making links between finding fractions of a set and dividing

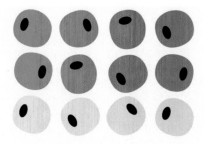

## Practice

1 a Can you use the picture of the beads to write a dividing sentence? Use the numbers 12, 3 and 4.

  b Can you write a different dividing sentence using the same numbers?

2 a Can you write another sentence for the beads picture that includes the fraction $\frac{1}{3}$?

  b Can you write a sentence for the beads picture that includes the fraction $\frac{2}{3}$?

................................................................................................................

## Going deeper

$10 \div 2 = 5$ and $\frac{1}{2}$ of $10 = 5$

1 Can you write sentences similar to the one above to describe each of these pictures?

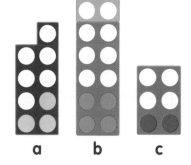

a    b    c

# Finding all possibilities

Amar is at a firework display. Three rockets are set off at a time. Some rockets make red sparks and some make yellow sparks.

## Practice

1 How many different combinations of red and yellow sparks are possible with three rockets? Can you find a way to record this?

2 How do you know you have found all of the combinations?

## Going deeper

1 a Other rockets make either red, yellow or blue sparks. How many combinations are possible with three rockets?

   b How do you know that you have found all of the combinations?

2 What would you tell a friend who didn't know how to solve problems like **question** 1? Can you write some hints?

# Finding all possibilities with coins

I have lots of each of these coins.

1p 2p 5p 10p 20p

## Practice

1 Can you help Tia find all the ways to make 20p? Find a way to record this.

2 What is the combination that uses the fewest coins?

3 What is the combination that uses the most coins?

4 Can you explain how you know that you have found all the possibilities?

## Going deeper

1 If Tia buys a sticker for 26p, which coins could she use? (Try to find the fewest coins first.)

2 Choose amounts under 20p and record all the different ways you can make the total using Tia's coins.

3 Is it true that you can only make even amounts with Tia's coins? How do you know?

# Investigating consecutive numbers

Some people call consecutive numbers "next-door numbers".

## Practice

1 Ben is thinking of three consecutive numbers. The largest is 8. What are the other two?

2 Find three consecutive numbers where two are odd. Can you find a pattern or rule for this?

3 Find three consecutive numbers with a product of 24. Is this the only answer? How do you know?

····································································································

## Going deeper

1 Can you find the total of these three consecutive numbers?

   a  14, 15, 16          b  11, 12, 13          c  24, 25, 26

2 Can you find three consecutive numbers with a sum of:

   a  21          b  15          c  9          d  27          e  18?

3 What do you notice about the answers to **questions 1** and **2**? Can you find a pattern or rule?

4 If you add two consecutive numbers together, will the answer always be even? How do you know? Can you explain your thinking to your partner?

# Investigating odd and even numbers

An even number plus an even number always gives an even total.

Ravi

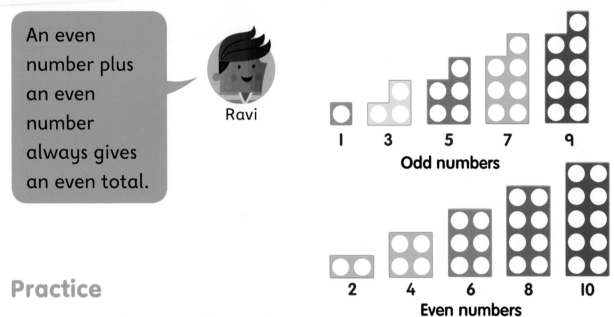

**Odd numbers**

**Even numbers**

## Practice

1 Is Ravi right? How do you know?

2 What happens when you subtract:

   a  an even number from an odd number

   b  an odd number from an odd number?

3 If you add three odd numbers, do you always get an even number? Can you explain?

## Going deeper

 1 Investigate these statements and say if they are true or false.

   a When four odd numbers are added together, they always make an even number.

   b The difference between any two odd numbers is an even number.

# Using position and direction instructions

## Practice

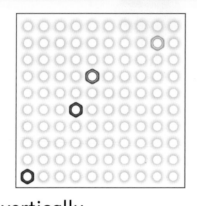
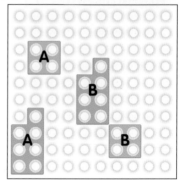

1 Can you write instructions to move the blue peg to the red peg? You can move horizontally and vertically.

2 Can you write instructions to move the yellow peg to the the green peg?

3 a Can you give instructions on how to move the 7-shape from position A on the grid to position B?

   b Now try this with the 4-shape.

   c Can you write instructions to move each Shape back again? What do you notice about your instructions?

## Going deeper

1 Place your finger on the top left corner of the left grid above. Find your way to each peg by moving horizontally and vertically. Now can you write the instructions you would follow to collect each peg?

2 Choose some Numicon Shapes and place them on a baseboard. Now place the same Shapes somewhere else on the board. Can your partner describe how to move the Shapes from one position on the board to another?

# Using compass directions

## Practice

1 If you are facing north and make a three-quarter turn clockwise, what direction will you be facing?

2 Look at the map.

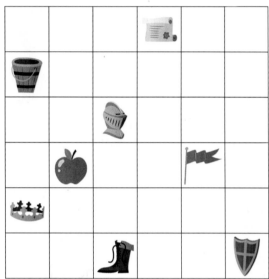

a What object is directly west of the shield?

b What objects are north of the helmet?

c What object is directly south of the bucket?

**Key**

scroll
helmet
flag
boot
bucket
apple
crown
shield

3 What can you say about the position of the flag in relation to the other objects?

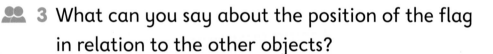

## Going deeper

1 Marta is standing on the square containing the apple and facing east. Can you write down what moves could she make to get to the scroll?

2 Using the map, choose an object as your starting position and tell your partner the direction you are facing. Can your partner tell you the moves you need to make to reach another chosen object?

# Using grid references

Harry is exploring his local area and uses this map.

## Practice

1  a Can you give the grid reference for where the train station is?

   b What park is directly east from the station? Can you give the grid reference?

2 Where does the river start and end on the map?

3 Can you name the building that is south of the golf club?

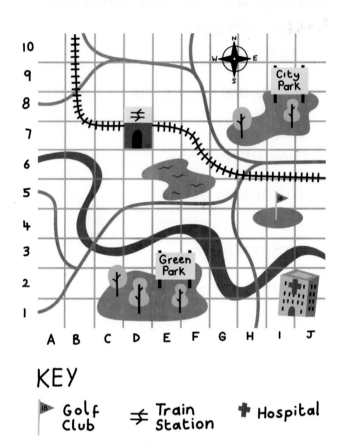

KEY

▶ Golf Club    ⚑ Train Station    ✚ Hospital

4 If you are standing in square F4 facing east and then turn a quarter of a turn clockwise, which park is straight ahead of you?

.........................................................................................................

## Going deeper

1 Can you use compass directions and grid references to ask your partner questions about the map?

2 Secretly choose a position on the map. Can your partner ask questions to work out where you have chosen?

**grouping**

Occurs in dividing when we know an amount and want to find out how many times a different amount will go into it, e.g. 2 goes into 10 five times. (See also **dividing, sharing**.)

**halving**

Dividing into two equal parts. (See also **dividing, grouping, sharing**.)

**height**

The measurement from top to bottom. (See also **length, width**.)

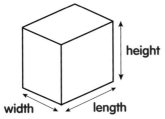

**hexagon**

A polygon with six sides. (See also **irregular polygon, regular polygon**.)

**horizontal**

A straight line parallel to the horizon. (See also **parallel, vertical**.)

**hour**

Sixty minutes. (See also **minute**.)

**increase**

To get larger in number or size. (See also **decrease**.)

**interval**

The distance between two points or the numbers between two values, e.g. the sequence 2, 4, 6 has intervals of 2. (See also **number line, sequence**.)

**inverse**

The reverse or the opposite. Adding and subtracting have an inverse relation to each other and each can undo the other, e.g. 8 + 6 = 14 so 14 − 6 = 8.

**irregular polygon**

A 2D shape formed of straight lines, which does not have angles all the same size or sides all the same length. (See also **regular polygon, quadrilateral**.)

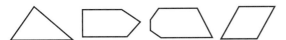

**length**

The measurement from one end to the other. (See also **height, width**.)

**less than**

Used for comparing values, shown by the symbol <, e.g. 2 < 4 shows that 2 is less than 4. (See also **greater than**.)

**mass**

The amount of matter in an object measured in, e.g. grams (g), kilograms (kg). (See also **volume, weight**.)

**method**

Way of finding an answer or doing something.

**millennium**

One thousand years. (See also **century, decade**.)

**minute**

Sixty seconds. (See also **hour**.)

**multiple**

The product of two whole numbers larger than one, e.g. 15 is a multiple of 3 and of 5, 5 × 3 = 15.

**multiplying**

Repeated adding of a number to find 'so many lots of something', e.g. 3 lots of 4 = 4 + 4 + 4 = 3 × 4 = 12. Also 'scaling up', e.g. scaling up a recipe for 2 into a recipe for 6. (See also **adding, dividing, product, scaling**.)

**non-unit fraction**

A fraction that is more than one part of the whole, e.g. $\frac{2}{5}$ or $\frac{3}{8}$.

**number line**

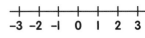

A horizontal line showing numbers (positive and negative) at regular intervals. It can extend forever in both directions.

**number rods**

Coloured rods of different lengths used for visualizing relationships and calculations.

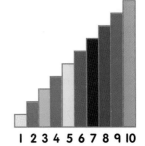

**number sentence**

A number fact that is written horizontally, left to right, e.g. 4 + 23 = 27.

**number trio**

A set of three numbers that are related together either by adding and subtracting, or by multiplying and dividing, e.g. 3, 4 and 7 are related by adding and subtracting. 4 + 3 = 7, 3 + 4 = 7, 7 − 4 = 3, and 7 − 3 = 4. (See also **adding**, **inverse**, **subtracting**.)

**numeral**

A symbol or group of symbols that represents a number. (See also **digit**.)

**Numicon Shapes**

Shapes of different sizes used for visualizing relationships and calculations.

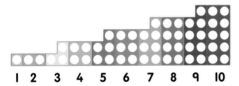

1  2  3  4  5  6  7  8  9  10

**odd number**

Any whole number that cannot be divided exactly by two. (See also **even number**.)

**pan balance**

When the masses on each side are equal, the pans will balance.

**parallel**

Lines that remain the same distance apart and never touch. (See also **horizontal**, **vertical**.)

**partitioning**

Splitting a number in different ways, usually to help with calculating, e.g. 27 can be partitioned into 2 tens (20) and 7 ones (7). (See also **bridging**.)

**pentagon**

A polygon with five sides. (See also **irregular polygon**, **regular polygon**.)

**perimeter**

The distance around a shape, e.g. the perimeter of this rectangle is 5 + 2 + 5 + 2 = 14

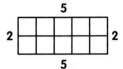

**perpendicular**

At right angles, e.g. perpendicular lines are lines at right angles to each other. (See also **horizontal**, **parallel**, **right angle**, **vertical**.)

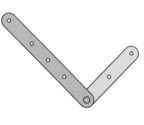

**place value frame**

A table with columns separating numbers into ones, tens, hundreds and thousands values, e.g. 8452 shown in a place value frame.

| Thousands | Hundreds | Tens | Ones |
|-----------|----------|------|------|
| 8 | 4 | 5 | 2 |

**p.m.**

The second half of the day, between midday and midnight. (See also **a.m.**)

**polyhedron**

A 3D shape with flat faces. (See also **3D shape**, **cuboid**, **face**, **tetrahedron**.)

**predict**

Work out what you think will happen.

**product**

The number resulting from multiplying two or more numbers together, e.g. in the multiplying calculation 6 × 4 = 24, then 24 is the product. (See also **multiplying**.)

## quadrilateral

A polygon with four sides. (See also **irregular polygon**, **regular polygon**.)

rhombus    kite    trapezium    parallelogram

## quarter

One of four equal parts of a whole. Can be written as $\frac{1}{4}$. (See also **halving**.)

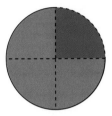

## recipe

A set of instructions for making something, usually food.

## regular polygon

A 2D shape formed of straight lines, which has angles all the same size and all sides the same length. (See also **irregular polygon, quadrilateral**.)

## remainder

Something that is left over when other parts have been used, such as the amount left over in a dividing calculation, e.g. $22 \div 5 = 4$ remainder 2. (See also **dividing**.)

## right angle

An angle of exactly 90°. (See also **angle**.)

## Roman numerals

Symbols used by the Romans to represent numbers, e.g. I = 1, V = 5, X = 10, L = 50, C = 100.

## rounding (up or down)

Increasing or decreasing a number or amount to make it closer to (usually) a multiple of ten, or a whole measuring unit, e.g. rounding 353 to 350 or 89 cm to 1 metre. Often done to make calculating easier, but less accurate. (See also **estimate**.)

## rule

A specific pattern or set of instructions to be followed. (See also **criteria**.)

## scaling (up or down)

Describes the amount by which something is increased or reduced to make it larger or smaller in proportion, e.g. when scaling up a recipe for 2 to a recipe for 6, you would multiply the quantities by 3.

## sequence

An ordered list of numbers, shapes or objects, e.g. 20, 25, 30... (See also **consecutive numbers, interval, term**.)

## set

A collection of objects or numbers.

## sharing

Occurs in dividing when we know an amount and how many equal parts it is to be shared into, but not how big each of these parts will be, e.g. 10 shared into 5 parts. (See also **dividing, grouping**.)

## short written method (for multiplying and dividing)

Written method for recording multiplying and dividing calculations. (See also **dividing, multiplying**.)

```
   1 1              × 1 5
 ×    6        3 )4 '5
   6 6
```

## side

Straight line joining the vertices of a polygon. (See also **edge, face, vertex**.)

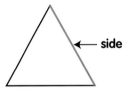

← side

## simplify (a fraction)

To reduce a fraction to the smallest numbers possible, e.g. $\frac{2}{4}$ to $\frac{1}{2}$.

## strategy

Way of solving a problem.

## subtracting

Taking one thing away from another, decreasing the size of something, or finding the difference between two numbers. (See also **adding, difference**.)

## symmetry

Objects or images with halves that mirror each other are symmetrical, e.g. butterflies, tennis courts.

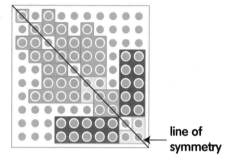

line of symmetry

## tally chart

A way to record counting by making marks on a chart.

**Votes for best flower bed design**

| Group | Tally |
|---|---|
| 1 | IIII |
| 2 | THL THL IIII |
| 3 | THL IIII |
| 4 | III |

## term (in a sequence)

One of the numbers in a sequence. (See also **sequence**.)

## total

Two or more amounts are put together to make a 'total' or 'sum'.

## tree diagram

A diagram used to sort items or to show all possible outcomes.

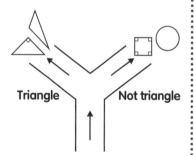

Triangle      Not triangle

## Venn diagram

A type of sorting diagram. (See also **Carroll diagram**.)

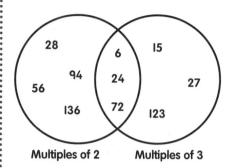

Multiples of 2      Multiples of 3

## vertex (plural vertices)

A point where two sides meet in a flat shape, or a point where three or more edges meet in a 3D shape. (See also **2D shape, 3D shape, edge, regular, irregular polygon, polygon, side**.)

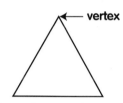

vertex

## vertical

A straight line at right angles to the horizon. (See also **horizontal, parallel**.)

## volume

How much space something takes up, often measured in $cm^3$ or $m^3$. (See also **capacity, mass, weight**.)

## weight

How heavy something is. (See also **capacity, mass, volume**.)

## width

A measurement from one side to another. When describing oblongs, the width is usually the shorter distance between sides. (See also **height, length**.)

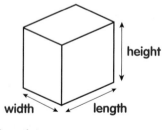

height, width, length